★ ★ ★ ★ ★ THE ★ ★ ★ ★ ★
TRANSITIONING
MILITARY
PROJECT MANAGER
Second Edition

THE TRANSITIONING MILITARY SERIES

THE
TRANSITIONING
MILITARY
PROJECT MANAGER
Second Edition

Jay Hicks, PMP
Lieutenant Colonel, United States Army, Retired

Sandy Lawrence, PfMP, PgMP, PMP

Foreword by US Congressman (OH)
Bill Johnson

GR8TRANSITIONS4U, INC.

GR8TRANSITIONS4U
Published by GR8TRANSITIONS4U
GR8TRANSITIONS4U (USA) Inc.
PO Box 2
Valrico, FL 33595

Hicks, Jay
Lawrence, Sandy
The Transitioning Military Project Manager
Includes End Notes
ISBN 978-0-9864376-7-0

Printed in the United States of America
Book design by Tamara Parsons
Kensington Type & Graphics

Dedicated to the Soldiers,
Sailors, Airmen and Marines
of the United States Military.

CONGRATULATIONS! If you have picked up this book, you are probably ready to embark on your military transition. You may be unaware of the significant project management experience that you have gained from the military. This book will assist with military transitional challenges and provide some good common sense guidance as you deal with the uncertainties and the associated ambiguities along your journey. By reading and using the tactics in this book you gain a professional advantage, setting into motion a course of action that will reduce transitional stress and create a satisfying and financially lucrative outcome.

Millions of service members have transitioned – now it is your turn. This book, along with its companion guide, will help you organize for your transition, ease your concerns and increase your confidence. Download your free companion guide from GR8Transitions4U. com. The guide contains copies of reusable assessments, charting forms and a personal strategic roadmap, in addition to process details and examples for using the forms. Keep the companion guide nearby and use it when performing the personal assessments and charting your strategic roadmap.

Leverage your military experience.

Good luck in your transition!

Table of Contents

Foreword

I first met Jay Hicks and Sandy Cobb at United States Central Command (USCENTCOM) while serving as a senior IT manager on a contract with Lockheed Martin. I was interested in bringing in a mix of military and industry experienced talent, and was fortunate to find Jay and Sandy. Sandy was a credentialed PMP with a no nonsense approach and great instinct on organizing a PMO, projects, and teams. Jay brought a wealth of project management experience from his many years of military service. Within 18 months, we established and chartered the PMO. Most importantly, they helped hire 13 more project managers - all who became PMP credentialed, and worked with them daily to establish a single voice to the customer

Their success soon led them to build other PMOs and help numerous employees become qualified and certified project managers. After a few years, they honed their method and wrote *The Transitioning Military Project Manager,* assisting a much larger audience - military personnel seeking quality civilian jobs during transition. This book helps in two ways: gaining knowledge of commercial project management; and, easing the associated challenges of military transition.

I have no doubt that you, too, can become a professional project manager; based upon your in depth specialized knowledge, and the unique leadership skills you obtained during your military service. You have managed projects while in the service, you have just used different terminology.

Relative to military transition, *The Transitioning Military Project Manager* offers a clear pathway to developing and implementing your personal strategic transition plan. Assessments and the subsequent planning documentation provided offer a superb method for executing the military transition.

I managed many major projects in the Air Force, which enabled me to advance my post-retirement civilian career from project to program manager, business owner, and eventually Corporate Chief Information Officer for a major publicly traded manufacturing company serving the transportation industry. Even more interestingly, my leadership and project management skills from the military and my early transitional jobs have assisted me on numerous occasions as a US Congressman.

I want to personally thank you for your military service, and I want to assure you that the military and veterans are at the forefront of my mind as I perform my daily tasks in the U.S. House of Representatives.

I commend *The Transitioning Military Project Manager* to you, and I wish you the very best in your transition - Godspeed.

Bill Johnson
Member of Congress

THE TRANSITIONING
MILITARY PROJECT MANAGER

1

Introduction

"WATER... WATER... EVERYWHERE. THE FATE OF THE CITY IS SEALED."[1] So the cry was heard throughout the day and night of August 29th, 2005. Katrina had taken the City of New Orleans. The wind was bad, but when the levee breached, the floodwaters were horrific. Eighty percent of New Orleans was underwater. St. Bernard Parish was completely submerged as billions of gallons besieged over 100,000 homes. Questions about how the devastation occurred are now immaterial. In the form of water, change had come to New Orleans. The city would never be the same again.

Rebuilding became the focus. Not surprisingly, an army of leaders, project managers (PM) and engineers were called upon to rebuild a stronger levee system. Many active duty and former military personnel answered the call to assist in the reconstruction of a devastated city. Former Vietnam era Sergeant John Bronson found himself in the center of the reconstruction effort, as he had become a lead project manager for the levee system rebuilding effort.

> "As water has no constant form, there are in war no constant conditions."
>
> Sun Tzu 孫子
> *The Art of War*

Like many young men and women in 1967, Sergeant John Bronson volunteered for service. Many years after his Army effort, John worked his way through civilian supervisory and project management positions. John was busy performing project management for a major corporation in 2005. Like most of us, he watched the weather closely during Hurricane Katrina, and had no idea that such devastation would be forth coming. Further, John was unaware of his imminent involvement with the reconstruction of New Orleans.

Why was John selected to be the lead project manager for the levee effort? He believes his success is derived from basic skills learned in the military. Along with his desire to excel, he believes that his project skills grew their roots while working with the 7th Infantry Division. John's number one axiom is that a project manager must understand every team member's job. Additionally, John understands the ability to adapt to the environment is a critical element. Traits such as leadership, discipline, flexibility, and planning are common to the military experience. These attributes are vital in civilian life just as they are in military life.

Change

Nothing is constant, except change. New Orleans changed. John's career changed on many occasions. Now you are going to change occupations and potential career fields. In today's tumultuous work environment, modern workers must be flexible, be able to adapt to change and reinvent themselves every few years to remain viable. The good news is that you have spent years learning to adapt in ever changing environments while in the military. You know that your military experience has instilled the ability to be flexible and given you the ability to respond to change.

Why Project Management?

Your future career path could very well be project management. Experts in the field believe that military are well suited for the career field of project management. Your leadership and planning skills ingrained during military service, and your adaptability to change, will enable you to successfully transition into a great career field like project management.

Action officer, training officer, operations planner, commander, platoon sergeant, are all military terms that equate to project manager in the civilian world.

That makes project management a high-value, target rich environment for you to consider. You may not fully understand the civilian terminology and methodologies, but you will be highly successful once you grasp these concepts and see how your military experience has prepared you for them.

Mark Langley, former CEO of the Project Management Institute (PMI), spoke directly to the project management opportunity for military personnel by stating that "...many veterans have project management experience – just under a different name." Your skill sets need to be translated and repackaged so that hiring managers spot your skills. Terms like "mission-related" often translate to "projectized". According to Mr. Langley, both the government and military are "highly projectized environments, which makes many veterans a natural fit in the project management world."[2]

Fortunately, you already know and understand the basics of project management. The military has exposed you to time management, how to work a multitude of simultaneous requirements, and how to get the job accomplished. Further, you know how to take charge when required, you are not afraid to lead, and you know how to talk to senior leadership. All of these essential project management skills that you have already acquired are discussed later as critical attributes and increase your understanding of commercial project management.

Another great advantage for you transitioning into this career field is the positive outlook for project management globally. The project management job market is expanding with growing opportunities and you are well qualified to compete. In a recent CNNMoney.com survey listing the top 50 best jobs in America, Information Technology project manager was ranked at number five. Along with job growth, there will be a significant increase in the economic footprint of the profession, and it is slated to grow exponentially. The Project Management Institute reports that approximately 16 million new project management roles will be added globally across seven project-in-

> *"Strategy without tactics is the slowest route to victory. Tactics without strategy is the noise before defeat."*
>
> **Sun Tzu 孫子**
> *The Art of War*

3

tensive industries by 2020.³ Thus, you can choose a career field that will offer great growth potential over the next few years. The outlook is indeed optimistic and should offer unfettered growth well beyond this timeframe.

Transition Strategy

As a military service member, you inherently understand planning and strategy. Your ability to plan and execute a personal transition strategy is potentially your greatest attribute. Knowing the tactics needed to get you to your goals and objectives are key. While transitioning from the military, you have to starting asking questions like:

1. How do I chart a course of action that will allow me to unleash my superb capabilities as quickly as possible after transitioning from the military?
2. Do I know my best qualities to exploit for my next career?
3. Do I know what career is best suited for me?
4. How do I get from where I am to where I want to be?

Your "Personal Strategic Roadmap" will assist in answering these types of questions, offering success in your career change by establishing obtainable goals and objectives. Interestingly, this process is quite natural for both the military mind and that of the project manager.

Why this Book is for You

Recommendations abound from well-meaning people telling you how to land your dream job, live your life, and enjoy success. In the midst of your transition, like in the fog of war, you can feel unbalanced and confused. It is easy to get lost and realize years later that you have chosen an undesirable path. It will become painfully obvious if you have not connected all the dots correctly. The only way to ensure a successful transition is to understand and apply the basics. Careful planning and execution are critical. Just like a military mission, plan well and execute brilliantly. Therefore, understanding your skills as related to basic project management concepts is vital. This book and associated materials will provide assistance in understanding project management and building your transition roadmap. Practical advice on how to take the skill sets that you have already obtained in the military and apply them to civilian project management will increase your confidence and help you to become a skilled and trusted project manager. If your transition has already begun, this book may provide answers to critical information you may have missed.

The Value of this Book

Most transition programs offer general guidance by means of generically creating a resume, interview tips, and similar features. You become acutely aware of the transition challenge, when you discover the uncertainties associated with career path decisions. It can take years to decide on a path if you do not have an understanding of who you are, what qualities and capabilities you offer, what you desire from life and where you desire to live. This book is uniquely suited to help you answer those questions and guide you to the best-suited career path for you and your family. Quality information and assessment tools in this book will help you evaluate your current situation and enable the development of a personal strategic roadmap for your successful transition. A series of personal assessment questions are provided in the areas of environment, characteristics, timing, skills, and desired market place. The assessment assists in the development of your strategic roadmap and guide you toward a potential career path in a marketable area that you and your family will find satisfying and rewarding. Further, this roadmap will prove invaluable as it has incorporated your motivations, skillsets and willingness to seek out the wide variety of opportunities in your next career as a project manager. This book and its tools will help you understand your strengths and weaknesses while increasing your professional skills and making yourself more marketable.

Conventions Used in this Book

Each chapter provides additional resources for your personal growth. Throughout the book, the Star Box (shown on the right) is used to call your attention to important facts to further research and use for transition. Sources vary from websites, book references, credentialing materials, or other programs and resources in the area of military or civilian project management.

Great Information Here

Know Yourself *(Chapter 2)*

Common challenges during your transition will be discussed. After thought evoking reviews of attributes and skills common to many in the military and high quality project managers, you will gain a greater understanding of this alignment. Additionally, you will explore transition timing, lifestyle desires, and risk tolerance. Multiple assessments covering personal and environmental desires are given to assist. Through these self-assessments you will gain a documented understanding of your desires as they relate to your transition. Spousal participation in this chapter is recommended, as any transition should be a team decision.

Project Management Basics *(Chapter 3)*

You have already performed project management, just not commercially. In this chapter, you will gain an understanding of the commercial vernacular needed to assist your transition and better position you for a career in project management. Types of project management methodologies are discussed along with why project management is a great job for you to pursue. You will gain an insider's perspective on career paths, sample job descriptions and corresponding roles/duties. Comparisons and insight on project management methodologies are given. For those wanting to gain that extra insiders edge, different types of certifications are explored to include cost, and expected return on investment. A cross-walk of terminology, resources and basics in project management will help frame expectations that you may be interested in pursuing. Through the skills assessment, your answers give you a realistic view of your potential alignment to the project management career field.

The Market Place *(Chapter 4)*

This chapter looks at three markets for project managers: Department of Defense (DoD) contracting, civil service and commercial (or corporate) environments. Obviously, there are significant differences between military and civilian markets. Many of the different characteristics are presented outlining pros and cons of each market. The marketplace assessment will help guide you through a process to assist you in determining your risk tolerance, job creativity, income needs, and stress levels.

The Right Fit *(Chapter 5)*

Assessment results will be organized and analyzed resulting in a personal index, unfolding your personal roadmap, mapping your best-suited transition path. Key indicators from your environmental, characteristics, skills, timing, and marketplace assessments will become clearly stated tactics supporting your roadmap. With this information and tactics in hand, you will be given options to pursue aligned with your strategic goals and objectives. Executing your Personal Strategic Roadmap will be key to finding and pursuing the best transition path and job based on your assessment results.

Appendices and Web Site

Our goal with this book is to help you assess and organize key facets of your life and experiences that will point you towards the best, most lucrative and rewarding career in project management. This book and supporting website provide a repository of easily accessible resources and experiences to assist you in your transition. Tools, assessments and templates are available in the appendices. Having purchased this book, you are also eligible for the Companion Guide, where reusable tools and templates are provided in electronic format online through the GR8Transitions4U.com web site.

Regardless of the path you choose, use this book and the associated assessment tools from each chapter, as a system to assist you in compiling your Personal Strategic Roadmap as a guide to finding the most effective course of action for your transition.

The only question remaining is: Have you thought of everything you need to make the right decision? Let's find out!

**Companion Guide
free at**
GR8Transitions4U.com

Sergeant John Bronson
Leveraging Military Experience

DURING THE VIETNAM WAR IN 1967, Sergeant John Bronson volunteered for service and ended up in Korea. With a good attitude and his military college experience, he was quickly promoted and became an operations non-commissioned officer (NCO) for the 7th Infantry Division G3 in Korea. On the division staff, he learned scheduling, management, the importance of goals and objectives, and the "Army" way of doing business. As he developed plans and orders, he began to hone his personal strategy and perform duties that would lead to a career in project management.

After leaving the service, John found himself back in the United States as a civilian looking for work. Using the GI Bill, he obtained a bachelor's degree, and soon began a career in the project related functions of planning, estimating, and quality control. Thirty-five years later John was engaged in the greatest challenge of his lifetime, rebuilding the levee system in New Orleans.

Due to John's tremendous project management reputation, he was asked by his corporate vice president to go to New Orleans for a couple of weeks and make an assessment of the situation. In 2012, John proudly stated that he had completed the project of a lifetime as a project manager in one of the United States Army Corps of Engineers' top efforts in history.

Shortly before John's arrival in New Orleans, Congress authorized a $14 Billion funding initiative known as the Hurricane Storm Damage Risk Reduction System (HSDRRS) for southeast Louisiana. John's project management reputation preceded his arrival and he was quickly engaged to correct a project that had gone awry.

John began to perform a series of quick fixes that included; realigning resources and skill sets, and re-baselining *project schedules. After fixing the levee plans, John personally project managed the steel and concrete gate structures for the 1.8-mile-long Inner Harbor Navigation Canal (IHNC)-Lake Borgne Surge Barrier, located about twelve miles east of downtown New Orleans. This massive structure reduces the risk associated with a 100-year storm surge for some of the areas hardest hit by Hurricane Katrina in metro New Orleans and surrounding parishes. The total construction value for the IHNC-Lake Borgne Surge Barrier was $1.1 Billion.*

Due to John's extraordinary project management skills, the IHNC reached the 100 year level of protection on May 22, 2011, nine days ahead of schedule. When Hurricane Isaac struck the greater New Orleans region on August 29, 2012, on the seventh anniversary of Hurricane Katrina, the flood protection infrastructure was put to the test and performed flawlessly.

John's leadership contribution led to the project receiving multiple coveted project management awards, to include the 2013 National Council of Structural Engineers Association Excellence in Structural Engineering Award.

2

Know Yourself

UNDERSTAND YOUR PERSONAL TRAITS AND CHARACTERISTICS THAT MADE YOU SUCCESSFUL IN THE MILITARY. Part of this understanding is an awareness of your personal environmental factors and a keen sense of timing in order to make your next move. Knowing yourself and exploiting your strengths are the best ways to acknowledge your level of readiness for transition.

This chapter is an exploration of you and why you are desirable as a project manager. The most successful transitions occur when you match your traits, attributes and characteristics to the job market. Identifying your undiscovered corporate abilities and applying them to your resume and interview performance will increase your probability of a successful transition.

As in any transition, analyzing the timing of your departure is a key factor. With regard to your timing, this chapter includes an analysis of many

> **"If you know the enemy and know yourself, you need not fear the result of a hundred battles."**
>
> Sun Tzu 孫子
> *The Art of War*

11

elements, such as studying the educational benefits, developing and refining your resume, making interview preparations and approaching certification as a project manager. Personal environmental factors are also a critical area that will be reviewed to help successfully understand yourself during your transition. Additionally, a brief look at common possible challenges and risks during this process are presented.

Honest introspection is not an easy task, but will prove valuable through this exercise. Three assessments are offered in this very important chapter to help gain insight to your level of readiness. They include:

- A **Characteristics Assessment** to gain an understanding of your military and undiscovered skills that will translate well to a career in project management.

- An **Environmental Assessment** that will challenge your understanding on outside factors such as location, retirement, family, schools and faith. If you are married or have a significant other, it is highly recommended you both take the assessment. Afterwards, discuss any results that might warrant more detailed analysis to offer better alignment.

- A **Timing Assessment** to determine how ready you are to transition based upon the availability of time for planning or need for immediate action.

Desirability of Military Personnel in the Civilian Market

Civilian employers find the characteristics and attributes obtained from your military experience invaluable. Transitioning military of all ranks have marketable technical and leadership skills. Beyond leadership, your military experience has enhanced numerous attributes or core competencies including loyalty, respect, integrity, reliability, and team building. From a military perspective, you have led teams and can adapt to many different situations rapidly. As a team player, you know the weakest link is someone who needs help keeping the team moving forward. Additionally, as part of a military group, you are educated and tech savvy, a quick learner, drug free, possess a security clearance, perform well under pressure, and are probably willing to relocate for advancement. These attributes make you very marketable to the commercial employer in the civilian market.[1]

Department of Defense (DoD) contract and civil service environments desire your military characteristics as well. Your contacts and understanding of military policy and procedure are vital to the defense contract organization. The bottom line is that you have many career options after the military, which are further discussed in Chapter Four. Your challenge is to consider job market opportunities and decide what you would like to do for your next career based on the proper alignment of your skills.

Your predecessors have instilled a reputation for high quality attributes developed through military service. In fact, over 30 million veterans have come before you since World War II. These veterans have laid the foundation of this reputation through their skills and abilities. You need confidence to know that your skills and abilities from the service are directly applicable to the project management job market. Translating these capabilities to the civilian employer is critical for your successful transition and the remainder of this chapter will provide assistance in this vital process.

Empirical Studies

You are probably aware that literally hundreds of companies are military friendly. The United States Automobile Association (USAA) hires veterans of all ranks and is perhaps one of the most veteran friendly companies in America today. Railroads such as Union Pacific and CSX have a tradition of being military friendly. Of course there are numerous defense contracting companies (L-3, General Dynamics, Booz Allen Hamilton, Lockheed Martin, CACI, etc.) that frequently hire former military personnel as well.[2]

Military Friendly Employers

Showyourstripes.org/ veterans

A survey was recently published by the Society for Human Resource Managers on the subject of employers and their thoughts on hiring former military personnel. The survey was given to Human Resource professionals from across many different U.S. based companies. The findings were startling. In general, companies felt that there are many benefits to recruiting and hiring veterans. The most commonly cited quality is a sense of responsibility and ability to see efforts through to completion. In fact, an overwhelming 97% of companies surveyed believe the veteran's strong sense of responsibility is their number one factor in hiring military.[3]

Discrimination Rights:
eeoc.gov/eeoc/
publications/ada_
veterans_employers.cfm

On the down side, some companies have misperceptions about the risks and challenges associated with hiring employees with military experience. Some companies feel that veterans are challenged working in a liberal work place. They are concerned about the misconception that former military employees will need extra time to adapt to new workplace cultures. A few companies have concerns about combat related disabilities. Another misperception that veterans are under qualified for the positions they are applying for. This is not the case! The challenge is for you, the veteran, to speak their vernacular to demonstrate your understanding of the job requirements. Thorough research of the companies and jobs you are applying for will provide the ability to demonstrate your knowledge of the position and how fantastic you really are.

Consider these misperceptions as you interact with recruiters and hiring managers. Understand their concerns and plan your answers to interview questions accordingly. By arming yourself, you will relieve concerns and frustrations during your discussions. Remember, the skills you have obtained in the past will carry you through your transition.

Personal Characteristics

Character is derived from the word characteristic. Both of these words refer to the essence of a person or thing. Character is the combination of qualities that makes us different from one another. Characteristics are made up of traits and attributes. Traits are generally innate. A person may be outgoing or reclusive -

shy or social. You likely still have some of the same personality traits that you were born with, even today. Traits are often difficult to change. However, all types of traits are needed in project management. You just need to figure out how your traits add value to your future employer.

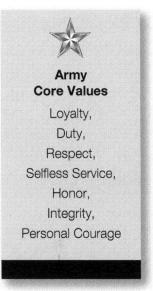

Army Core Values

Loyalty,
Duty,
Respect,
Selfless Service,
Honor,
Integrity,
Personal Courage

Attributes, as opposed to traits, are not ingrained. Attributes are learned over time and are based on external experiences. Attributes generally refer to a specific behavior or behavior(s). Therefore, as a military service member, you may have developed strong attributes during a challenging and difficult professional career or situation, such as combat or peace keeping operation. Attributes such as motivation and enthusiasm are examples of characteristics that may change with your life or professional experience. A person may be committed or have strong integrity. He or she may be loyal or hard working. These attributes lead to certain behaviors, which can be strong predictors of how one will respond to different stimulus in the work environment.

It is essential to know your traits and attributes as they define your personal characteristics and character. Understanding yourself to this level will help you determine what best suits you in a career. For example, do you enjoy working with other people or prefer working alone? If you enjoy organizing efforts and leading a group, you may be well suited for project management. You need to know how well you perform under stress. Your time in the service has shaped you, through the installation of military Core Values, so use these to your advantage. Military Core Values are well understood and appreciated by employers. It is essential to understand how the military service has shaped you and your attributes. Let's explore and use this knowledge for success in your next career.

Coast Guard Core Values

Honor, Respect,
Devotion to Duty

Core Values

Navy / Marine Core Values
Honor, Courage, Commitment

In addition to your attributes, you have been well indoctrinated into your services core values. Whether you are Army, Navy, Air Force, Marine, or Coast Guard, you have valuable attributes that can be applied in the job market. Some veterans have managed people, computers, or weapon systems. The common desirable theme among former military is their core values.

People hear the words Loyalty, Duty, Respect, Selfless Service, Honor, Integrity, and Personal Courage all the time. Service members learn these values during their initial training. During your military service, you practiced these values every day in everything you do, 24 hours a day, seven days a week. These values are tremendous attributes. The question is: How do you relay these to the prospective employer? It is likely that employers consider hiring former service members because they believe they have these attributes. However, you will still need to demonstrate your individual traits and attributes. Knowing yourself is the first step in doing so.

In addition to your core values, your traditional military qualities such as professionalism, leadership, confidence, positive attitude, communications and organizational skills are all highly desired by commercial companies. Understanding your strengths and applying them to your job search and your career choice is key for your next job.

Why You Are Desirable As a Project Manager

Know that many of these core values and characteristics discussed are exactly what is desired of a quality project manager. This is not a coincidence, as old fashioned leadership is essential in project management. Arguably, some of the finest leaders in the world have been trained by the military. CIO.com and other organizations have provided opinions of the best attributes for project man-

Air Force Core Values
Integrity First, Service Before Self, Excellence in All We Do

agers.[4] Figure 2.1 below cross-walks the top project management attributes to similary military vernacular you have already heard and obtained.

QUALITIES OF TOP PROJECT MANAGERS	MILITARY VERNACULAR
Foresight	Ability to read the situation - "Good Read"
Know how to lead	Leadership - "Lead, follow or get out of the way"
Good communicators	Briefing and addressing unit -"Silver tongue" "Golden pen"
They're pragmatic	"Cool under Fire"
They're empathetic	Understand how to motivate others
Quick sifting abilities	Getting to the facts, quick learner
Set, observe, and re-evaluate project priorities	Make a decision, even if it's wrong! "Adjust fire if necessary"
Ask good questions and listen to stakeholders	Quick learner, educated and tech savvy
Predictable communication schedules	Training schedules, briefing schedules
Consensus-building skills	Team work - "Do or die", "Get it done
Informal networks	Team Building - "Buddy system"
Look forward to going to work	Devotion to Duty -"Gets the job done"
Organized	Professional – "Got his stuff together"

Figure 2.1 | PM to Military Cross-Walk

By virtue of military service, you already know how to track issues on a daily, if not hourly, basis. These two organizational qualities are key for any successful project manager. You have had to reassign tasks to other service members, take or give fitness tests, and oversee weapons cleaning; all simultaneously. It has been said that the difference between project success and failure is based on whether the project manager is highly organized. Are you?

Stress

You are battle hardened and have been through many trials and tribulations. Many of you have worked in very stressful and time sensitive environments, including combat zones. As you enter a new job market, you will face other types of trials and tribulations. However, most civilians have not experienced the challenges that military lifestyle brings. You should be confident about your ability to deal with difficult situations. Stress in the corporate world is meeting profit objectives. The stress you have experienced is different and comes from wondering if the abandoned car beside the road is an Improvised Explosive Device (IED). Stress is stress, but they are not all the same and you have to develop a new understanding of stress in the civilian sector and confidently realize "I got this".

Project Management and Stress

Many project managers cite stress as the main downside to their jobs. PMs are responsible for their projects' successes or failures, which determine both their income and status within a company and industry. In construction, if a project isn't brought in on time, the contractor has to pay damages for each day's delay, and the project manager could lose a bonus and possibly even his or her job. Juggling the triple constraint (cost, schedule and scope) proves a daunting task. However, for some looking for a challenge and wanting to see the mission completed, the black-and-white nature of project management work makes for a refreshing challenge. Delivering a project "on time and under budget" can provide great emotional rewards. The job offers the opportunity to lead and new projects keep the work fresh. If you have an analytical mind, good people skills, the desire to see a job well done and work well under pressure, this may be your next career.

Preparing mentally to deal with stress during your transition is essential. Stress will present itself during transition from home work and seeking a new job. You will need to deal with transitional responsibilities that arise prior to your departure while the office will have an expectation that you will continue to work. However, you must take the time to do preparatory activities such as; assembling a resume, branding and interview practicing. These activities, along with a potential family move with school age children can cause significant personal and marital stress. Finally, the job hunt can take its own toll with stress. Knowing how to cope with stress is very beneficial during the transitional period. For example, if you like to work out, stick with it. Take time for your stress reducing activities. It can make the difference between a smooth or painful transition.

Your Undiscovered Corporate Skills

In addition to all of the previously mentioned characteristics and values, you have numerous undiscovered abilities. Left undiscovered, a prospective employer may fail to see desired capabilities.

Everyone is born with innate gifts and talents. Some of these you perform so easily that you hardly notice. Many of your finest qualities go unnoticed by yourself and others (Figure 2.2). A reflective

Potential Undiscovered Skills

Understanding group dynamics

Ability to read the weather and predict storms

Always knowing and speaking the right words at the right moment

Knowing how to bring an individual back into the conversation

Understanding how to bring a group of people back into harmony

Loving the challenge of a puzzle

Motivating a group with low moral

Sensing direction, never lost

Figure 2.2 | Potential Undiscovered Skills

question here is, "Have you taken the time to study what you are naturally good at and where you excel?" Are you a great communicator? Do you know how to push people to get a job done? How about motivating or mentoring others? All of these abilities assist in making a great project manager. This introspection will allow you to see what others observe and how you can capitalize on these abilities as you transition from the military to project management.

Often, people overlook some very good non-work capabilities such as hobbies, travel, cars, etc. Someone may be a great fisherman and feel that this is of no consequence in the work environment. They may have a tremendous understanding of when and where the fish will be biting. You may say, "Who cares about when and where the fish are schooling?" This can be parlayed into conversation openers to break the ice in project meetings, getting SMEs to work for you in a non-projectized organization, or just getting to know your sponsor. This communication technique is commonly used with customers and sponsors. The best way to establish and gain consensus from stakeholders is by connecting with them on a personal level. Next time you go into offices of a customer or hiring manager, look at the photos or items on the wall and try to figure out what this person is about. Inquire on something you see, positively and open mindedly. You may very well find that you may have similar background or experiences. This is frequently how new relations begin.

Do not under estimate any personal attribute that you have. Start with discovering what makes you unique and what defines you. List these out. Understand how they can assist you in the job market and at the office. Some of these capabilities may be added at the top of your resume for personal attributes, which will be discussed later in the resume section of this chapter.

The bottom line is that you may have many undiscovered traits, characteristics and attributes. These may be learned or may be innate. Regardless, they are invaluable to you and your future employer and should be resume highlights (Figure 2.3). Recognize these features, understand their qualities in the workplace and try to apply them. Take the time now to study those skills and how they can be of value to your future employer.

There are three assessments in this chapter. Use them to gain an insight on your personal factors to include capabilities and potential growth areas.

Resume Attribute Bullets

Motivational leader

Planner and problem solver

Concerned and caring manager

Excellent group dynamic skills

Enjoys solving challenging complications

Figure 2.3 | Resume Attribute Bullets

Assessment #1 *(Personal Characteristics)*

This assessment explores your personal readiness and preparedness for transition. You may answer the assessment questions here. When you are ready to analyze your answers, refer to Chapter Five. Remember, the Companion Guide at GR8Transitions4u.com is available for you to print all assessments found in this book.

Figure 2.4 requires you to analyze your personal characteristics, traits and abilities. Choose one answer for each question given.

1: Personal Characteristics

	Strongly Disagree	Disagree	Neither Agree OR Disagree	Agree	Strongly Agree
I enjoy working with and being around people.					
Collaborative efforts are more desirable to me than working alone.					
I tend to lead a group when given the opportunity.					
I can perform well in a stressful environment.					
I adapt quickly to changing environments.					
I enjoy being part of a team effort.					
I have the ability to learn concepts quickly.					
I prefer working with others from different backgrounds and different skill sets.					
I take pride in briefing and reporting on my work.					
I proactively desire to learn and experience new concepts.					

Figure 2.4 | Personal Characteristic Assessment

Personal Environmental Factors

As you begin your transition, it is important to understand your personal environmental factors. These factors affect you, your family, and your job opportunities. If you are like most, you will work after you transition from the military. If married, you certainly need to take into consideration your family's environmental requirements as you make decisions. Therefore, ensure you work through this section with them. If single, some of the considerations listed here may be relevant to your extended family or future plans.

> *"...success is to be measured not so much by the position that one has reached in life, as by the obstacles which he has had to overcome while trying to succeed."*
>
> ~ Booker T. Washington

Family and Health

As you transition, you need to consider your special family needs. Being close to extended family may constrain your job searching to certain geographic areas. Proximity to airports and hospitals might also require consideration.

There are many family issues to consider during your transition. Does your spouse need or want to work? Can they find jobs at the location you desire? Will he or she require more training or education? Will you or your family need to be near a university or college? Have you studied or discussed sharing your Post 911 G.I. Bill benefits with your family?

A few questions you should consider are:

- Do you have access to medical care or a Veterans Administration hospital?
- Do you understand the impact on you and your family regarding the loss of military benefits?
- Do you know how much risk you and your family are willing to take with your next position?

Work-Life Balance

Another environmental factor to take into consideration as you transition is your Work-Life Balance (WLB). You have worked hard in the military. Part of the assessment process is understanding where you reside on the WLB continuum. When looking for a job you should consider work-life attributes such as the demands that your occupation will require. Are you ready to climb the corporate ladder? You may find a demanding job and make a lot of money, but is that what you want for your retirement job? Occasionally, you can find a job with great WLB and make lots of money. However, if you make $120,000 you should generally expect to put forth a $120,000 effort.

A good WLB makes for better health and happiness (see Figure 2.5). You can work hard and make a lot of money, but inadvertently affect your health and/or family life. Your personal investment in knowledge and experience will allow you to achieve greater expertise, accomplishment, fulfillment, and financial reward. However, it is easy to get caught up in a cycle of hard work and reward. Be cautious, as a successful career must have balance or one will burn out personally, professionally, or both.

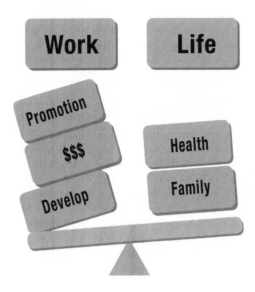

Figure 2.5 | Hazards of Work-Life Balance

Location

Location, Location, Location! - A phrase we are all quite familiar with. A critical consideration is moving to the location of your choice prior to your transition. It can be challenging and very expensive to get back to your U.S. home or to your desired location on your own dime, especially if overseas. You can save a tremendous amount of money if you can have the military move you back to your home of record, or if you can take your last assignment at your desired location. Another advantage to making this happen as part of your transition or retirement would be the ability to begin building your future local network early. If you know where you are going to end up, begin building your network remotely. Here are a few other questions you should ask yourself if you have not already:

10 best places for military to retire:
livability.com/topics/community/10-best-cities-for-veterans

- Have you considered the location of your next job?
- Have you looked at the climate as it relates to your health, hobbies, and personal activities?
- What is the unemployment rate?
- How many government-related jobs exist in the local area?
- What is the cost of living?
- Do you have the need or desire to be near a military base so you can use the commissary, exchange and other facilities?
- Are you looking for a rural or urban life experience?
- Do you wish to live overseas?

Assessment #2 *(Environmental Factors)*

The goal of assessment #2, presented in Figure 2.6, is for you to perform a personal analysis of the associated environmental issues with your transition. As with the first assessment, read each question and choose the best answer. Refer to Chapter 5 when you are ready to analyze the results.

2: Environmental Factors	Strongly Disagree	Disagree	Neither Agree or Disagree	Agree	Strongly Agree
I have performed a post-military financial analysis, to include the loss of military benefits if applicable.					
I have determined my desired geographic location with regard to such factors as healthy lifestyle, allergies, health care access, hobbies, weather and entertainment.					
I have considered my family's special needs in my transition planning.					
I have analyzed and understand myself with regard to work life balance.					
I have given thought to my future location with regard to military base and/or VA Hospital proximity.					
I have studied transition locations with regard to extended family and transportation hub.					
I have analyzed my transition location with regard to future employment, taxation, real estate cost, and overall cost of living.					
I have considered my spouses occupation and their ability to find work.					
I have taken into account my children's primary, secondary and/or college education requirements.					
My family is supportive of my transition into another career.					

Figure 2.6 | Environmental Factors Assessment

Timing

As the saying goes "Timing is everything." As in any transition, timing is a key factor. Are you ready to leave? Do you have to leave? Are you satisfied with your military efforts and ready to move on? These questions are mixed to ascertain your level of readiness to transition from the Service. With regard to your timing, this section includes an analysis of many elements, such as studying the educational benefits, developing and refining your resume, making interview preparations, and approaching certifications. The following timing related topics are presented as rhetorical questions for your comprehension, personal review and self-organization.

Is the Timing Right?

Are you ready to go? You do not want to regret your transition, as there is no going back if you still have something left to do in the military. There are many things to consider about timing. Your gut instinct is probably not the best method for this determination. Looking at the associated timing issues and conducting self-assessments will likely provide you with a better result. These decisions should be made with a clear head and strong conviction. You may not be able to choose when to leave the Service, but you can choose to prepare yourself as completely as possible. The bottom line – prepare the best you can with the limited time you have. Below are some things to consider when deciding if the timing is right to leave the Service.

Are You Having Fun?

This may sound silly, but are you having fun in the military? Only you can determine if you are enjoying your military duty. In general, active duty personnel truly enjoy the military lifestyle and the associated excitement. Many people look back at their time in the Service and remember their experience fondly. Others look back on their military Service as an accumulation of tough days. However, you should expect to have tough days in your civilian job as well. Some will remark, "Wow, did I do the right thing by getting out?" Just remember, the grass is not always greener on the other side of the fence.

Have You Achieved Your Personal Goals for Military Service?

Achieving your personal goals in the military can be quite challenging, especially in today's world. You may have specific goals you were trying to obtain that are no longer attainable. You may also have a brilliant career ahead of you. Making the decision to get out of the Service is always difficult. If you have accomplished your primary goals and objectives for military Service, there is no need to fret about whether you should stay any longer. You may be aware that you have obtained the highest rank possible. Remember, there is a point where you will no longer get selected for promotion. The Congress continually adjusts the size of the military based on the needs of the nation and the defense budget. The Services have had to reduce their end-strengths in the past, are doing so now, and will do so again in the future. During these personnel draw-downs, everyone undergoes assessment and some will be involuntarily released from active duty. If this is your situation, be prepared and transition in a positive manner.

Has A Good Transitional Job Opportunity Presented Itself?

Many veterans have stepped out of the Service straight into great jobs. This occurs with some degree of frequency, but it is not the norm. Often your first job is "transitional." After being out a while, you realize that your first job is probably not the one you truly desire. Remember, it is acceptable to test the waters when you first get out. Regardless, if you desire to grow and develop you may have to move on.

Not everyone will have a job in his or her back pocket when initially transitioning. The question that you should ask yourself is "Am I taking all the appropriate steps for a job opportunity to present itself when ready?"

Are You Prepared to Leave the Service?

Education and Certification

Can you list your skills and education? Are you comfortable with this list? Do you want or feel the need to acquire more? The

"When opportunity comes, it's too late to prepare."

~ John Wooden

company that hires you does not always provide skills and education training at the onset. You must be ready to step in and work. Organizations occasionally offer training; however, you may need to sign an agreement to pay back the training fees or commit to an additional time period. The military is a great environment for training and learning because of all the educational programs and opportunities available. Generally, every branch of Service offers some form of military tuition assistance while on active duty. This lucrative benefit goes away upon transitioning and should be used prior to your departure from the Service. Further, you may be able to get the Service to pay for specialized related certification training before departing. Each Service has on-line guidance for credentialing and certification. Pursue these avenues with a great diligence before departing the Service.

Shortly after your transition from the Service, you should obtain a Post 911 G.I. Bill certificate of eligibility from the Veteran's Administration. This is the essential starting point for using this tremendous educational benefit for you and perhaps your family's education.

Post 9/11 GI Bill
benefits.va.gov/gibill/
post911_gibill.asp

You may be eligible for this VA-administered program, if you have at least 90 days of aggregate active duty Service after September 10, 2001, and are honorably discharged or were discharged with a service-connected disability.

How is Your Financial Readiness?

Have you saved enough money to survive the transition period? These dollars need to be in short-term savings and not locked up in a retirement account in order to avoid tax-related penalties. For many, the question is, "How much should you keep in a 'rainy-day' fund?" According to the Bureau of Labor Statistics (BLS), an acceptable measure of three to six months' worth of expenses may no longer apply. Ryan Guiana, author from *The Military Wallet*, suggests shaping your emergency fund to equal three to six months of your monthly expenditures, not your salary. [5]

Have You Prepared Your Resume?

There is a tremendous amount of information available to assist military veterans in the preparation of their resumes. This book is not intended to be a definitive guide on resume building. However, this guide provides discussions on enhancing the communication of your brand and methods of avoiding common resume "landmines" or pitfalls frequently encoun-

> *"Whoever said the pen is mightier than the sword obviously never encountered automatic weapons "*
>
> ~ General Douglas MacArthur

tered by your fellow Service members. Remember, a powerful, impactful, well-written resume using commercial and business language, combined with the right format and branding power, can set you apart and propel you to a rewarding position in the private sector. Your resume and cover letters are your personal calling cards. To create a well branded and powerful resume you will need to go beyond providing your job description.

Be aware that commercial and civil service resumes can be very different. A few years ago, it was best practice to create a special resume with a specific format when applying for civil service positions. However, with the development of USAJOBS.gov, you can now upload your resume to this website and no longer use a resume builder for civil service jobs.

Your Military Experience is Unique!

Many transitioning Service members have challenges talking about the uniqueness of their military experience with the hiring managers. You must capitalize on the extraordinary capabilities that you have achieved while in the Service. You will need to speak to the value and difference you made while serving in each position. Capture the size, quantity of personnel, and if appli-

Need resume assistance:
resume-place.com/
veterans/

cable the multiple geographic locations that you had to coordinate with and/ or synchronize associated with each position. You will need to talk about the impact and volume of what you routinely handled.

Resume Writing: Art and Science

There is a definite skill to writing a resume. It is an art to speak about yourself and connect your value to the value desired by a company. It is a science to include the key terms in your resume so a computerized search engine can identify those words within your resume and put it at the top of their pile for consideration. There are many tools and books to assist you with this.

"Be Bold. Most of us have a sense of humility, but a resume isn't the place for it."

~ Anonymous

You will most likely need to write and re-write your resume multiple times. Be smart with your network; use military friends and colleagues who have transitioned well for a civil servant position. Use other networking groups from professional or other non-military organizations for commercial insight and guidance. You will need to modify the resume until you are comfortable with it. If you are challenged with resume writing and have money for professional preparation, this may be a good investment.

It is recommended to post your resume on hiring sites like Monster.com, Indeed.com, and Career-Builder.com. These sites are scanned on a regular basis and you will get frequent emails informing you of potential opportunities. Even if the job is not exactly what you desire, apply! In addition to potentially gaining a greater appreciation for the company and associated career opportunities, the interview experience is very valuable.

Superb tools for automatically translating your occupation skills to civilian jobs!
military.com/
veteran-jobs/skills-
translator

Resume Format

Impact! When your resume gets in front of a recruiter or hiring manager, it has approximately twelve seconds to do its job. It needs to be clear and error-free and most importantly, show your value! The three major formats presenting their values are listed in Figure 2.7, below:

29

Resume Type	Description
Chronological	Starts by listing your work history, with the most recent position listed first. Jobs are listed in reverse chronological order – with current, or most recent job, first. Employers typically prefer chronological, easy to see jobs held and when worked. Works well for job seekers with strong, solid work history.
Functional	Focuses on your skills and experience, rather than on your chronological work history. Used most often for changing careers or gaps in employment history.
Combination (Hybrid)	Lists skills and experience first. Employment history is listed next. Highlights relevant skills to the job you are applying for, while providing chronological work history that employers prefer.

Figure 2.7 - Resume Types

Employers tend to favor a resume that is easy to follow and clearly communicates your professional track. If you plan on writing your own and have 10 or more years of experience and education, select a format that concentrates on your assignments, your accomplishments (value), and education. A great guide for specific resume examples and templates can be found in *"The Military to Civilian Transition Guide: Secrets to Finding Great Jobs and Employers."*

Resume Formats:
www.thebalancecareers.com/job-resumes-4161923

Common Resume Pitfalls

The following errors in resume writing are often found in Service member resumes as they prepare for transition. Avoiding these problem areas will increase the probability of your resume getting through the HR staff screening and into the hands of the hiring official.

Service Member Jargon

There is no place for military jargon or vernacular in your civilian resume. Terms such as command and control, tactics, ISR, execution of battle plans, OPTEMPO, and weaponry mean nothing to a civilian recruiter and are insignificant. This is also true for unit names or assignment locations. Write your resume with the target audience in mind. Most of the people scanning it are HR professionals who understand their industry and recruiting, not mortar ranges and targeting of terrorist networks. Focus on plain business language and your potential value to an employer. Remember, many years of military Service and the word "retired" may arouse undesirable assumptions.

Very Long Resume

A resume should be two pages or less in length. Do not try to cram 25+ years of military Service into the resume. Instead, adjust your format and focus on your last 10-12 years. Employers will thank for you for this.

> *"Be so good they can't ignore you."*
> ~ Steve Martin

Resume with No Direction

"Operations manager, sales manager, director of business planning and jack-of-all-trades." Do not let your resume display uncertainty or ambiguous career goals. Your resume should not float between work experience narratives with no central focus. You need to make a decision and decide what you want to place in your objective statement and write your resume to that. You can always change your mind with the next version of your resume or have multiple resumes, but you should focus on one career direction per resume. Remember, you are telling a story and creating a brand for yourself. Your resume must show direction and tell your personal story as it relates to the position for which you are applying.

Job Duties Only

Often a Service member's first cut on a resume focuses on the job duties performed. This makes sense as these are easily transferred from your military evaluations. However this technique does not work. Remember, you are your own best salesman! You need to focus on achievements and the impact you made to show value and worth to your potential employer. By only listing job duties, you are telling a prospective employer you do not bring much to the table other than following directions. If you lack documentable educational degrees, make sure to highlight your professional development training and associated certifications.

Your resume needs to show how you can help provide value from the company's perspective in areas such as financial goals, strategy, market penetration, or process improvement. Demonstrate you are more than an employee and that you are an asset to any team. Believe it or not, everyone else competing for that same job knows this secret!

Getting to the Top

How do you stand out? Getting your resume to the top of a hiring managers list among hundreds of candidates will be challenging. You obviously want your resume to be noteworthy, but you do not want to look arrogant or inexperienced. You must be understood by hiring managers, which can be a difficult task for anyone in transition. Here are a few pointers:

Customize for the Intended Audience

As you transition, you must be flexible and versatile. Make sure your resume is appropriate, as every company and position is different. Therefore, you may need several different versions of your resume; each emphasizing different facets of your career objectives and achievements. Be consistent and do not contradict yourself.

Get to the Point

Consider integrating the specific job posting title into your objective statement. Do not present a high level, generalized and vague comment about how you are looking for a challenging position with a dynamic company as an accomplished professional. Describe your pertinent experiences and qualifications in quick and energetic terms.

Don't Over Embellish, but Tell a Great Story

Recruiters expect a resume to reflect an element of spin, but over exaggeration is detrimental. Shine the most favorable light on yourself and your achievements. However, excessive embellishments may keep you from getting hired. If hired, you run the risk of being placed in a position where you are under-qualified and cannot perform well.

Integrate Keywords from the Job Posting

Today, keyword search is a screening criterion. Do not overdo it, but ensure keywords are present in your resume. This is critical for all online applications and resumes as most are screened by computer search engines. Further, you may receive subsequent contacts for positions that you have not applied for. Do you satisfy the criteria on the job posting? If so, do you reflect that on your resume? Get the keywords on your resume.

Avoid "en vogue" Terms and Words

Your resume should not read as if has been pulled from the latest business magazine or thesaurus. Forget over-used words and phrases; try to be original. However, do not overuse big words when simplistic language will do.

Remember, there is no Jedi mind trick to influence your selection by a HR recruiter. Sending out resumes is a matter of trial and error. You must keep submitting and experimenting with different formats and approaches until something works for you. With ingenuity and realistic expectations, you will create a bulletproof resume that represents well and lands you a great job.

Professional Branding

You are a professional brand. You might not necessarily realize this fact when you begin your transition, but it is true. Your resume, LinkedIn® profile, and job applications should all mutually support your common brand. Focus on key items like leadership or a subject matter expertise. Build a brand foundation that resonates throughout the resume. It is important to ensure your professional experience and education reflects who you are. Prospective hiring officials should have no doubt on your level of expertise and what you bring to the table. Make sure your Facebook and LinkedIn pages are strictly professional and synchronized, as hiring professionals look at them.

Achievements

Focus on both your achievements and career history, while highlighting your measurable capabilities and impact on the organization by personifying and enhancing your professional brand. A two-page resume should contain enough power when written well. You must show the impact you made on all previous positions. Listing that you had a job without any impact is wasting valuable resume space. Remember, they are hiring you and what you can bring to the table.

Cover Letter

Experts in the placement field say that the well-written cover letter... not the resume... will land more job interviews. As a transitioning Service member, it is a tragic mistake not to spend the time and effort necessary for a personalized cover letter, each time you submit an application. So, the question is can you rapidly construct a great cover letter? Here is some advice for constructing a great cover letter.

Be Brief

A short, pithy, excited and to the point cover letter will get your cover letter read. HR and hiring managers are not going to read through a long boring document, when they are quickly scanning for the right candidate. Often, less is more.

Layout

Remember to address your cover letter to someone! Find out who will receive the cover letter and address your cover letter to them. If you cannot get this information, open with a subject line like: "Cover Letter: Your Name, Your Credential." Remember, open the cover letter with a hook. The first sentence must grip the reader and will almost guarantee your cover letter and resume get a much closer look. You can do this through one of several methods.

- **Excitement** - You can express your excitement for the job opportunity. This translates to motivation and dedication. This can make HR want to find out more about your qualifications.

- **Using Keywords** - Knowing that scanning or applicant tracking systems are widely used, another approach to the opening line is to make it keyword-heavy.

- **Name Dropping** - Using a connection is a foreign concept to many Service members, because we don't do this in the military. If someone in your professional network refers you, don't hesitate to drop the name, straight away. This is frequent occurrence in the commercial world and people often receive referral bonus for doing so. Remember, time is money and this method helps HR rapidly fill positions with quality candidates.

- **Current Event** – Your cover letter opener can impact employers by demonstrating your knowledge of recent news associated with the company and relate that to the position you are applying for. Let them know why you would be the best candidate as relative to this news.

Make sure your cover letter communicates what you can do for the business, how you will benefit the company and its bottom line. You may need to take a few minutes and perform some internet searches to relate your added value in clear terms.

Ensure you have an enthusiastic ending and request something. Ask the employer for action. Go ahead and request an opportunity to interview this week or at their earliest convenience. Thank them for the opportunity. Your closing should assume you are going to land the interview.

T&T - Transportable & Tailorable

You want to be able to modify and reuse your cover letter repeatedly. So, you need to create a digital folder for cover letters. You need to be able to quickly tailor the opening and letter body to relate your skills to the essential elements of each job announcement. Don't forget to save your cover letter each time for quick modification and future use.

The cover letter is your marketing sheet; its primary purpose being to get job interviews. The more interviews you attend, the wider range of opportunities you will receive. Remember, applying and interviewing for jobs is a career-long process and it takes lots of practice.

Got Interviews?

Practicing interviewing is essential. Interviewing is like fishing – you need to practice. If a resume is your bait and hook, use the interview to reel them in. Seek out and go on interviews regularly just to stay in practice. Interviewing is a very special skill. It takes time and practice to hone your responses to the questions that your future employer will likely ask. Additionally, always be prepared to ask the hiring supervisor questions as well. This is a good indicator that you have done your homework and are showing an interest in what they do. Ensure you have studied the position description before the interview, so you can ask clarifying questions and gain more insight. Be honest during the interview. Do not overstate your capabilities. If you find you are not selected, you can and should ask why. If you make a mistake, you want to know so you can keep from making the same mistake again. Remember the adage: practice makes perfect. You can also inquire about other opportunities they know of within or outside their unit.

> "*I AM ... two of the most powerful words. For what you put after them shapes your reality.*"
>
> ~ Anonymous

Can You Communicate Your Characteristics to the Hiring Manager?

Communication is critical when dealing with a hiring manager. Normally, you will only get a few minutes with them. Most will sum up an applicant within the first five minutes. This is the opportunity to tell them what is not on the resume. Let them know you are the best candidate for the job. Huge dividends will be paid to the candidate who, prior to the interview, learns many details about the company and its operations, their future supervisor, and the hiring manager.

After you have written your resume and find yourself in an interview, make sure you approach it with enthusiasm. Interlace discussions of your skills, flexibility, military traits, passion and trustworthiness to the hiring manager. Use personal experiences that resulted in positive end-states. Always communicate your best characteristics reflecting the attributes you have. It is time to unfold your story with enthusiasm and relevance to the company. Hiring managers view this positively.

Crafting an Elevator Speech
mindtools.com/pages/
article/elevator-pitch.htm

Finally, unless specifically asked, never speak about your shortfalls. However, be prepared to answer the question, "Tell us about a time you failed." These are great opportunities to explain challenges that you have experienced. It is not about the change or failure that happened, it is how and what you did after to carry on and learn from it. What is important is to show how you turned the situation around for the good and future results. You need a great answer in your hip pocket that indicates you learned from the experience.

Have You Developed a Network?

Developing your network is a two-pronged attack. One must have a local network and an internet network. A great way to develop local networks is to volunteer at your local military association such as the Navy League, Association of the United States Army (AUSA), or Armed Forces Communications and Electronics Association (AFCEA). However, getting off the installation and meeting with local organizations is a better way to expand your network. Find your closest Toastmasters Club. By way of example, the Tampa Bay Area has over 51 Toastmasters Clubs. The Project Management Institute (PMI) has chapters in over 110 cities in the United States and 237 chapters around the world. Additionally, there are numerous other professional organizations that you can get involved with around the country and potentially in your local area. Get started with the sampling of networking organizations presented in Figure 2.8 on the next page. These organizations and associations will not only offer national meetings, but often conduct regional and local chapter meetings. Each one of these groups actively seeks volunteers. Volunteer and you will not only grow in your understanding of the commercial professions and enhance professional skills; you will also actively increase your network. Some of these organizations offer certifications, which will be discussed more in Chapter 3.

PMI is one of these professional networking organizations that promotes the professional development of Project Management Professionals in the com-

Organization	URL
Agile Alliance	www.agilealliance.org
American Society of Transportation & Logistics, Inc. – ASTL	www.astl.org
APICS - supply chain and operations management	www.apics.org
Armed Forces Communications and Electronics Association	www.afcea.org/site/
Association for Computing Machinery (ACM)	www.acm.org
Association for Project Management (APM)	www.apm.org.uk
Association of Information Technology Professionals (AITP)	www.aitp.org
Association of Shareware Professionals (ASP)	www.asp-software.org
Computer Professionals for Social Responsibility (CPSR)	www.cpsr.org
Council of Supply Chain Management Professionals	www.cscmp.org
Independent Computer Consultants Association (ICCA)	www.icca.org
Institute for Supply Management – ISM	www.ism.ws
Institute of Electrical and Electronics Engineers (IEEE) Computer Society	www.computer.org
International Association of Public Health Logisticians (IAPHL)	www.IAPHL.org
International Society of Logistics – SOLE	www.sole.org
National Association of Programmers	www.napusa.org
Network Professional Association (NPA)	www.npanet.org
Optimist International	www.optimist.org/
Project Management Institute (PMI)	www.pmi.org
Rotary International	www.rotary.org/en
Scrum Alliance	www.scrumalliance.org
Society for Human Resource Management (SHRM)	www.shrm.org
Software Development Forum (SDF)	www.sdforum.org
The Academy of International Business	www.aib.msu.edu
The Academy of Management	www.aomonline.com
Toastmasters	www.toastmasters.org
Veteran Mentor Network	www.veteranmentornetwork.org
Warehouse Education and Research Council	www.werc.org
LinkedIn Groups	
Construction Project Management	https://www.linkedin.com/groups/3776031/profile
PM Community	https://www.linkedin.com/groups/1770182/profile
PM Link	https://www.linkedin.com/groups/59531/profile
PMI Military Liaison	https://www.linkedin.com/groups/6798540/
PMI Project, Program, and Portfolio Management	https://www.linkedin.com/groups/2784738/profile
Prince2 & MSP	https://www.linkedin.com/groups/51931/profile
Project Management Professionals PMP	https://www.linkedin.com/groups/83310
Project Manager Community	https://www.linkedin.com/groups/35313/profile
Project Manager Network	https://www.linkedin.com/groups/37888/profile
Project Transition USA	https://www.linkedin.com/groups/4842096/

Figure 2.8 | Professional Organizations and Associations

mercial environment. PMI supports the profession by providing a community of practice where members network and improve their professional skills. PMI seeks to advance the project management profession through standardization and professional development with support of education and advocacy.

Just as important as developing a local network is developing your virtual network. On-line professional networking companies such as LinkedIn® are invaluable. Keeping in contact with friends and acquaintances through LinkedIn® is easy. Social media outlets are a great way to receive the latest news and opportunities.

Find local Toastmasters
Toastmasters.org

Further, members keep their addresses updated so there is no need to update your address book. This is a perfect method for keeping up with your professional acquaintances. If you have not done so already, build a LinkedIn® account and start building your online network as soon as possible.

EverNote® is another great application that works with your smart phone and LinkedIn®. Simply snap a photo of the business cards you collect from con tacts and it automatically feeds your LinkedIn® Account. It is a great concept as more and more folks join LinkedIn®. The bottom line is that you need to network. It will pay huge dividends as you depart the Service. Remember to start early.

Transition Assistance Program

Finally, have you attended your local transition assistance program? These programs are essential for teaching you the basics needed for a successful transition. Transition information and counseling for pre-separation, employment assistance, relocation, education and training, health and life insurance, finances, reserve affiliation, disabled veterans, and retirement are provided. However, do not expect to find a job from this program.

Military Transition Web Sites:

Air Force:
www.afpc.af.mil/Retirement/

Army:
sfl-tap.army.mil/pages/transition/
preseparation_timeline.aspx

Navy:
public.navy.mil/bupers-npc/career/
transition/Pages/TAP.aspx

Marines:
usmc-mccs.org/cycle/transition/

Coast Guard:
https://www.dcms.uscg.mil/tap

SWOT Analysis

As another tool for your transition preparation and ability to know yourself, the Strength, Weaknesses, Opportunities and Threats (SWOT) analysis is presented. The SWOT analysis was originally developed for strategy and marketing and is used extensively by business developers. SWOT is a method for determining competitive advantage in the market place. Use this tool to help determine your competitive advantage to the job market competition. Performing a self-analysis to determine your abilities or challenges within these four areas will not only give you a greater understanding of yourself, but will also provide a level of confidence needed to be competitive. Figure 2.9 below depicts those characteristics or attributes common to military personnel based on their typical military experience.

Strengths	Weaknesses
Internal, positive aspects under your control to exploit:	Negative aspects you control and can improve upon:
Military work experience (Ch. 2)	Lack of commercial work experience (Ch. 3)
Education (Ch. 3)	Lack of understanding of job market (Ch. 3)
Technical knowledge (Ch. 2)	Lack of commercial vernacular (Ch. 3)
Transferable characteristics - communication, leadership, teamwork (Ch. 2)	Negative self-image (Ch. 2)
Personal attributes - ability to work under pressure, work ethic, etc. (Ch. 2)	Dealing with negative misconceptions about military service members (Ch. 2)
Innate Military Core Values (Ch. 2)	Not understanding how to become marketable (Ch. 3)
Ability to assess and perform introspection on your capabilities (Ch. 5)	Lack of commercial experience or career knowledge (Ch. 3)
Ability to gain certification (Ch. 3)	
Opportunities	**Threats**
Positive, external conditions outside of your control that you can exploit:	Negative, external conditions you cannot control, but can reduce the effect:
Career field growth (Ch. 1)	Knowing your competition (Ch. 3)
Military friendly companies (Ch. 1)	Negative misconceptions about former military (Ch. 2)
Opportunities available through further educational and certification (Ch. 3)	Competitors with better job hunting capabilities (Ch. 2)
Funding of school through GI Bill program (Ch. 3 & 4)	Obstacles - lack of education and/or certification (Ch. 3)
Fields in need of military attributes (Ch. 2)	Competitors with superior skills (Ch. 3)
Opportunities available with greater preparation and self-knowledge (Ch. 3)	Failure to stay marketable (Ch. 3)
Opportunities by greater understanding of commercial career field and market place (Ch. 4)	
Networking with seasoned Professionals (Ch. 3)	

Figure 2.9 | SWOT Analysis

Assessment #3 *(Timing)*

In assessment #3 (shown in Figure 2.10), you will look at personal preparedness and timing of your transition. As before, read each question and choose the best answer.

3: Timing	Strongly Disagree	Disagree	Neither Agree or Disagree	Agree	Strongly Agree
I I am ready to leave the military experience behind.					
I have met my career goals for the military.					
I am enjoying or looking forward to making plans for my military transition.					
My resume has been completed and reviewed by a civilian professional.					
I have established a network of professionals in and out of the service.					
I have saved several months salary for financial sustainment during transition.					
I have successfully attended a local military transition assistance program.					
I have successfully branded myself on LinkedIn, Facebook or with appropriate professional associations.					
I have practiced my interviewing skills.					
I have performed a personal SWOT analysis.					

Figure 2.10 | Timing Assessment

Summary

Knowing yourself is critical when competing in today's job market. Seek professional enhancement at every turn. Do not be afraid to reach out to new opportunities and analyze alternative paths. Try different angles and exploit those areas where you get traction. Above all keep moving forward, no matter the challenge. The story below depicts a former soldier who was resilient in the face of adversity in combat and civilian job market.

Donna Keydash
Believing in Yourself

The first time Donna Keydash ever said she wanted to join the Navy was in 1976, at the age of 7. She told everyone that would listen, "When I grow up, I want to be a Sailor, just like my Dad!" Donna's father was stationed on a destroyer, based out of Baltimore. Unfortunately, her dad had to tell Donna that they didn't let women on destroyers. That did not faze Donna, as she retorted it wasn't fair. Knowing Donna would not permit her sex to be an obstacle to reach her personal goal, she enlisted in the Navy twelve years later, served aboard multiple destroyers, rising in rank to Chief Petty Officer (CPO).

During Donna's various tours in Navy Communications, she served for the Joint Chiefs of Staff, Division Chief, and supervised network, communications, and the cybersecurity of two Spruance-class destroyers—the USS Kinkaid (DD-965) and the USS Fletcher (DD-992). In the war, she managed cybersecurity as the Force Information System Security Manager (FISSM) for all of the west coast aviation command, including six carriers. Donna's culminating assignment was that of managing the cybersecurity of multiple Special Operations Forces (SOF) commands under Naval Special Warfare Group One (NSWG-1). Constantly learning and growing, Donna attended many military training classes and schools in the areas of data processor, database management, system and network administration, and communications security, among others.

Donna believes the military taught her leadership, teamwork, management, accountability, planning, follow-through, communicating (written and oral), scheduling, and attention to detail; all key attributes that would prove invaluable to her later in project management.

Donna's 20 year Navy career provided considerable experience directing and managing projects on a day to day basis, whether information technology related or special projects. Many aspects of her jobs aligned with project management processes, process modeling and data flowcharting. Donna's duties familiarized her with system development and life cycle management, certification and accreditation, which follows milestone processes like planning, analysis, design, and implementation.

A key to Donna's successful transition was achieving her Bachelor of Science in Management Information Systems in 2014 from the University of San Diego, prior to leaving the Navy. This educational exposure offered Donna a bridge between military technical jargon and the vernacular used in the business world, through business scenario application, vice military operations. Donna took a course in project management as she finished her degree. She asked herself, "Can I do this?" and answered, "Yes, it's just like being a Chief." Through Donna's personal contacts, networking, and building a solid reputation within her peers and leaders, she was interviewed for a DoD contracting project management position at United States Naval Special Warfare Command (NAVSPECWARCOM) or NAVSOC. Donna quickly accepted the position, which she finds very enjoyable and rewarding.

*A critical lesson learned by Donna is that you can have process, planning and documentation, but sometimes **"nothing goes as planned"**. Donna believes that a well structured plan, documented throughout the life of the project, is critical for future lessons learned. However, Donna also realizes that it is important to fully understand the requirements, identify more than one course of action and adapt to change. She believes in keeping communication lines open and ensure everyone is informed and up-to-date on progress. Finally, know that **"the job is not complete until it's documented"**.*

Constantly pushing forward, Donna is currently scheduled to take her Project Management Institute PMP® exam next month as it would give her credibility and validate the professional direction she intends to pursue. Retired CPO Donna Keydash believes the certification will be a testament to her professional knowledge, provide a code of ethics, and demonstrate her dedication to the profession of project management.

3

Project Management Basics

"...MANY VETERANS HAVE PROJECT MANAGEMENT EXPERIENCE – JUST UNDER A DIFFERENT NAME."[1] As you prepare for your transition, one thing is certain: the more you prepare and understand yourself, the higher the probability you will impress your new company. However, preparing and learning will get you only so far, because if you cannot translate your message into something meaningful the employer wants, it will not matter. Utilizing a different vernacular, you have performed projects many times in the military. This is crucial information to share with your future employer, and you need to understand and speak the civilian project management vernacular to ensure success.

The purpose of this chapter is to enhance your understanding of the exciting project management career field and provide you the basics of project management, while aligning your existing skills and capabilities to your future career pursuits. You will be able to "talk the talk" using your newfound civilian project management vernacular.

> "The reason the enlightened prince and the wise general conquer the enemy, is foreknowledge."
>
> Sun Tzu 孫子
> *The Art of War*

While there are numerous standards, papers, books and guidance on the field of project management, this chapter provides benefit as an insider's guide to the basics, correlating duty and performance, to the commercial market.

This chapter is organized into three sections.

1. *"Background"* – provides a brief history of project management in relation to its military origins and the military acceptance of commercial project management.

2. *"Understanding Project Management"* – provides a rudimentary understanding of the different occupations and introduces organization project structures.

3. *"Understanding Agile Project Management"* – delivers a high level understanding of Agile and the ever increasing prevalence in the work environment.

4. *"Way Ahead"* - presents a look into your future as a PM by providing an understanding of the career path and certification process through commercial training (free or low cost to you by virtue of your military service).

Later in this chapter, there is a skills assessment, which will determine your readiness for transition based on your knowledge of project management. Additionally, your personal growth areas in project management are highlighted, then addressed and monitored through your Personal Strategic Roadmap, presented in Chapter 5.

Finally, a key aspect of transitioning from one career to another within project management is gaining a comfort level by using the terminology transcending all industries, from military to information technology, healthcare, banking, and construction, to name a few. To help with this, we offer the following aids through our Appendices:

- **Appendix A** - A basic "Lexicon" is provided to enhance your understanding and relate key concepts from military to civilian terminology.

- **Appendix B** - A "Rosetta Stone" provides a cross-reference to the civilian market place, translating military planning processes to the project management process groups.

Background

Project management has been around for years. This section describes the maturation and ongoing trends within this career field as they relate to you, the transitioning military project manager.

Project Management Warfighter Origins

Project management is in your military DNA. You have used the same techniques for planning and execution of deployments, exercises, training missions, construction efforts, and large scale planning efforts like the Panama Canal.

Construction of the Panama Canal started in November 1906 was one of the first major, modern military project management efforts. President Roosevelt selected the Army Corps of Engineers to finish the canal work and appointed Major George Washington Goethals as Chief Engineer in February 1907. Major Goethals used techniques on this project, which eventually became part of modern project management.

Goethals would establish the first work breakdown structures (WBS) in history by dividing up the division of labor and duties.

Of further interest, the Planning for the D-Day Invasion in 1944 was a massive project with a multitude of plans, sequels and branches within a plan. General Eisenhower, the Supreme Allied Commander, stated that D-Day was "A project so unique as to be classed by many scoffers as completely fantastic. It was a plan to construct artificial harbors on the coast of Normandy."

Figure 3.1 offers some of the most notable military project management efforts, with the formation of several professional project management societies born in the late 1960s and early 1970s.

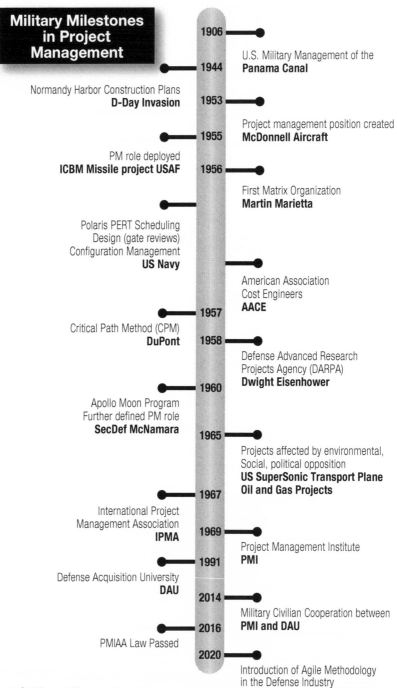

Figure 3.1 | Military Milestones in project management

Strategic Shifts in Civil Military Cooperation

Military and civilian corporations have continually evolved and enhanced project management, shifting emphasis from engineering to focus on delivery, communications, scheduling, skills, and costs. As more companies implemented these new techniques, people began attending seminars, conferences, and similar events to learn from one another and share their experiences. During this time, several professional project management societies were born and are now fusing efforts with the military.

Project management continues to expand and develop in the commercial sector. Now, through civil military cooperation, the military is again embracing and utilizing mature project management methodologies. There is a hunger within the military for knowledge and understanding of the project management career field as evidenced by the following strategic shifts.

PMIAA
www.congress.gov/bill/114th-congress/senate-bill/1550

On December 14, 2016, the President signed bill S.1550 -- the Program Management Improvement and Accountability Act of 2015 (PMIAA) into law. This piece of legislation was fully supported by the Project Management Institute (PMI) and garnered staggering bi-partisan support. The act is designed to reduce waste and bring more rigger to current military and government project and program management practises.

Another commercial introduction is the advent of Scrum and Agile Methodologies. In the last decade, Agile is growing in acceptance not only by the Defense Department and development centers, but also in mainstream project management.

PMP® Skill Identifiers – Army and Navy

Over the last few years, the recognition of commercial project management within the military has spawned the creation of new service skills specifically for acknowledgement of PMI certifications. For example, the Army, in April of 2013, approved a Project Management Professional (PMP) skill identifier for engineer officers known as "W5". One year later in 2014, the Navy added coded designations and descriptions for PM roles.

Sample government & military project management guides and instructions:

dla.mil
acq.osd.mil
jcs.mil/Library/CJCS-Manuals/

Guides, Instructions, Handbooks

Many Government and military departments are standardizing project management methodologies and tools. DoD, Joint Chiefs of Staff, Secretary of Defense, National Institute of Standards and Technology (NIST), and numerous other Government agencies are offering instructions, guidelines, and standards to assist in Program and project management efforts.

If you plan on staying in the DoD work environment, you should become familiar with some of these handbooks. Some of these deal with specific subject matters such as Work Breakdown Structures, Integrated Master Plans, Risk or Earned Value Management.

Understanding Project Management

Simply put, project management is all about setting and achieving attainable goals. Project management is the method of planning, organizing, motivating team members, and controlling resources to achieve specific end states. It is a very dynamic, three-dimensional chess game utilizing standardized procedures and protocols.

Business managers oversee a specific functional business area, whereas PMs orchestrate all aspects of time-limited, discrete projects. As a PM, you may oversee the development of a new product or service or may manage folks from disparate departments like marketing, IT, and human resources.

Business management operates in a continuum. Traditional, also known as waterfall project management, is usually finite in length, one-time pieces of work involving a number of activities that must be completed within a given time frame, and often on a fixed budget. Common examples of traditional projects are construction of a building, introduction of a new product, installation of a new piece of machinery in a manufacturing plant, creation of a new software tool, or the design and launch of a new advertising campaign.

Everyone practices project management to some degree. For example, farmers plan what, when, and how they're going to plant; how they are going to manage their crops as they grow; and how and when to harvest those crops. Parents plan what to prepare their children for dinner. Parents delegate, monitor and control tasks to children, like setting and clearing the table.

In business, project management is part art, part science - a skill and demanding full-time job. PMs are key employees with career paths in such industries as construction, engineering, manufacturing, and government. But, many opportunities for PMs exist outside these areas. For example, high tech, biotech, and pharmaceutical PMs are responsible for launching new products, developing new technologies, and managing alliance programs with strategic partners.

Seeing the Forest AND the Trees

While the simplest of projects can be successfully managed by applying common sense, complex projects require a great deal of planning, communication, and benefit from a formal, disciplined management approach. PMs are expected to take an uncertain event and make a certain promise to deliver. This is what makes project management so interesting and demanding.

Whether a project involves releasing a product, building out a new office site, or launching a rocket, your job as a PM is to make sure everything comes together in a timely, cost-effective manner -- and take the heat if it does not. This high profile, high-risk work demands multitasking ability, analytical thinking, and excellent communication skills.

A PM must also have current operational awareness and see future actions and risks simultaneously. To obtain this broad style of awareness, you must understand what is going on in your organization while maintaining and controlling all internal project related activities. To obtain an understanding of future actions, you must learn to look beyond the day, the week, and the milestones to foresee and anticipate future risks and expected outcomes.

Your greatest challenge as a PM is to achieve all of the project goals and objectives while respecting the predetermined constraints of scope, time, quality and budget. To be considered exceptional, you need to optimize delivery of all associated tasks to gain the utmost efficiency for your organization, thus maximizing profits, while keeping all stakeholders informed.

A Day in the Life of a Traditional Project Manager

Generally, as a PM, you will oversee planning, communications, implementation, quality control, and status reporting on a given project. You will manage your project team, which typically consists of people from all areas of the organization. Precisely defining the scope of the project, preparing the schedule, and updating that schedule as it evolves, proposing the budget, and managing the project so that it doesn't cause cost overruns are all significant responsibilities of the PM. Other responsibilities may include ensuring supplies are on hand when they are needed; that human resources are available to support the efforts necessary to get the project done on time and within budget; identifying and minimizing potential risks to the project timeline and budget; ensuring all project team members understand their responsibilities; communicating the project's progression to management; dealing with contracting, and ensuring quality.

PMI has defined five lifecycle processes within the Project Management Body of Knowledge (PMBOK).[2] Interestingly, if you manage multiple projects, you could be in various lifecycle process stages simultaneously. The following sections offer a glimpse of these phases and their meaning. Many books and standards have been written to explain the details and logic behind project management and its concepts, and can be found on the Internet or at your local library.

PMI®
Process Groups:

- Initiating
- Planning
- Executing
- Monitoring & controlling
- Closing

Initiating

The number one purpose of this phase is to ensure the stakeholders' expectations are aligned with the project's desired outcome. To do this, the PM must make sure the project charter and scope documents are properly defined. It is during this phase that definition of the left and right boundaries of the project are distinct as they shape and determine the deliverables what will define completion of the project.

One of the greatest challenges during initiation is determining what the end goal or project completion will be. Project closure occurs when the stakeholders' authorized and agreed-upon expectations and requirements have been met. If this end-state is not successfully agreed, the project scope may change and the project will never close. This seems to happen frequently in an environment where the customer is not educated on project management. Therefore, another critical task during this phase is educating the customer on roles and responsibilities, if necessary.

Other recommended tasks to assist in project success are the development of a cost benefit analysis and a Rough Order of Magnitude (ROM) costs, as well as the formulation of risk and mitigation procedures.

Planning

The number one factor in successful project management is the quality of the plan. This phase delineates the method and the course of action to successfully complete the project.

Thorough planning uses detailed planning for the short-term with a longer-term view emphasizing periodic reviews, re-planning, and risk management. This results in a project plan that can adapt quickly to abrupt business and deliverable changes with minimal impact to delivery schedules.

Too many times, projects start before completing the plan. Often this leads to project failure. Sometimes management does not realize the value of a project plan in saving time, money, and many problems over the course of the project.

However, more project information is understood as the project matures, thus requiring additional planning. Through the use of progressive elaboration, planning and documentation are somewhat iterative and gain fidelity as the project proceeds. The project plan is the required output of this phase and it will draw upon the numerous aspects of schedule, time, cost, communications, human resources, quality, procurement and their mitigation.

Scheduling

While not considered a formal phase, scheduling is performed throughout a project lifecycle, most notably in the planning phase. Scheduling is a way to communicate what tasks need to get done, by whom, and when.

Scheduling software programs can help in the task of resource allocation, another large aspect of a PM's job. For example, if you are running a software development project, you have to know how many engineers will be available and how many hours they'll need to work. Likewise, if you're running a construction project involving cranes and excavators that must be leased on an hourly basis, you'll need to know when to have those machines on site at the appropriate time to conserve project funds. Conversely, you also need to know how many days you can have the equipment on site without an overrun on budget. Good balancing of limited labor, materials, and other resources is a difficult task.

Executing

Highly skilled PMs that have mastered successful project execution earn top dollar and have a great reputation. The key elements of this phase include all efforts that are performed to complete the work in accordance with the project management plan while delivering the expected project results (deliverables and other direct outputs). Typically, this is the longest phase of the project management lifecycle, where most resources are applied. It is possible that during execution, the plan may require updating or re-base lining. The key elements of project execution are the ability to work effectively with the team while remaining faithful to project scope during unpredicted events and difficulties.

Changes in expected duration, unanticipated risk or resource challenges may drive some of these changes in schedule. Regardless, stakeholders and sponsors must be constantly informed of any change that occurs to ensure quality customer relations. To enable monitoring and controlling of the project during this phase, you will need to implement a range of management processes. These processes help you to manage time, cost, quality, change, risks and issues. They also help you to manage procurement, customer acceptance and communications.

Monitoring/Controlling

Racing the clock, grappling with the unknown, and simultaneously trying to contain costs is the PM's lot in life. So if there is one "magic elixir" that PMs need more than any other, it is control. Control means being able to systematically define customer objectives and the work required to fulfill them. Additionally, it means being able to time-phase the required work and measure progress towards completion. Further, anticipating future work-performance obstacles while responding effectively to them is critical.

"Monitoring and Controlling" is the fourth life-cycle phase of project management. The term "control" is included because execution is not a blind implementation of what was written in advance, but also a watchful process. This "control" is an integral part of project management and is a necessary task of the PM.

Closing

Project closure is very important as every team needs to dot all the "I's" and cross all its "T's" in a project. Like paperwork, some find it easy to lose interest and procrastinate finalizing a project, especially when another project is more interesting or is more demanding. If you have ever needed a previous project's documentation, you will understand the value of a quality closure. You want to make sure that a smooth handover is completed for all of the deliverables. This is essential because you do not want the client coming back to you at a later date stating that a piece of the project was not completed. If there are deliverables that are not completed at closure, each item must be clearly specified with a get-well date. Generally, the project sponsor will not allow closure until all of these deficiencies are worked off. Additionally, all sub-contract work has to be closed out. All financials need to be reviewed to ensure that all costs have been captured and vendors have been paid and their work is complete. You will need to perform final reporting and give a determination on how well you have performed against the baseline schedule originally established. Most organizations will want you to assist in capturing lessons learned with your project. All documentation needs to be captured in a repository, as it is essential to archive all technical specifications and documentation related to the project. These documents will be needed for future use and become essential if problems arise at a later date.

Teamwork and Communication

In today's world of unprecedented competition, organizations are being forced to simultaneously support one-to-one customer relationships and mass-customize their products and services. To succeed in this environment of extremes, success demands cross-functional teamwork and impeccable project management. Unfortunately, not all team members are as well rounded and well versed in effective project management as the situation often requires. Without properly skilled personnel and best practices helping them to make fast, business-savvy decisions, projects will fail.

A project's very survival – let alone its success - hinges on teams working effectively. Without cross-functionality and communication, the mix of skills needed to identify risks and reduce errors will be missing. Without communicating, risks that are obvious to one team member will not be communicated to other team members – often the ones most dramatically affected by the impact of the risk.

Traditional Project Management Frameworks

This section provides an understanding of different project management related structures and frameworks that are common within organizations. It is essential to understand the differences between the structures within this career field, maturity of these structures, and how you will fit and work in these structures.

Projects, Programs, and Portfolios

As with any new position, understanding terminology can be a daunting task. Understanding the differences and nuances associated with projects, programs and portfolios is important as you begin your journey into this career field. In many sectors, you will hear some or all of these terms used interchangeably. It can be confusing, even for the educated or credentialed. All of these entities provide benefit to an organization, by generating business value, enhancing current capabilities, facilitating business change, maintaining an asset base, offering new products and services to market, or developing new capabilities for the organization. The challenge is to understand how the terms are used within your organization because there is some variety and they are often used interchangeably or inappropriately.

Project

A project is temporary in that it has a defined beginning and end in time and therefore, defined scope and resources. The end is reached when the objectives have been achieved or when the project is terminated or no longer needed. A project is unique in that it is not a routine operation, but a specific set of activities designed to accomplish a singular goal.

Projects deliver outputs, discrete parcels or "chunks" of deliverables, typically defined through a WBS. A PM's job is to ensure that their project succeeds and keep the stakeholders informed of challenges that will affect schedule, cost or quality.

Program

Programs create outcomes and are comprised of components either non-project or project based. Programs can be nothing more than either a large project or a set (or portfolio) of projects. Additionally, programs work to exploit economies of scale and reduce coordination costs and risks. A program manager's job is concerned with the aggregate result of benefits realized for the organization.

PMI Project Definition:

A temporary endeavor undertaken to create a unique product, service, or result.[3]

For example, in a financial institution, a program may include one project that is designed to take advantage of a rising market, and another to protect against the downside of a falling market. These projects are opposites with respect to their success conditions, but they fit together in the same program. A singular project might deliver a new factory, hospital or IT system. By combining these projects with other deliverables and changes, programs might realize and deliver increased income from a new product, shorter waiting lists at the hospital or reduced operating costs due to improved technology.

PMI Program Definition:

A group of related projects, subprograms, and program activities that are managed in a coordinated way to obtain benefits not available from managing them individually.[4]

Project Portfolio Management (PPM)

PPM is the centralized *management* of processes, methods, and technologies used by PMs and Project Management Offices (PMOs) to analyze and collectively manage a group of current or proposed projects based on numerous key characteristics.[5] The objectives of PPM are to determine the optimal resource mix for delivery and to schedule activities to best achieve an organization's operational and financial goals – while honoring constraints imposed by customers, strategic objectives, or external real-world factors. The portfolio is one of the key indicators that reveal an organization's true intent, direction, risk tolerance, and progress.

PPM aims to determine the best grouping and sequencing of projects to achieve organizations' business goals, in order to see them through from concept to completion. Projects are typically analyzed based on the nature of the objective, expected benefits and costs, resource consumption and their relationship to other priorities within an organization's wider portfolio of projects.

Often, organizations will implement PPM software tools to aid in the decision-making process. PPM tools are used to enable visibility, standardization, measurement and process improvement. A strong IT governance structure is considered a crucial component of a project and portfolio management strategy as well. Most companies will work projects then

PMI Portfolio Definition:
Project, programs, sub portfolios, and operations managed as a group to achieve strategic objectives.[6]

realize they need to organize them into programs and portfolios to achieve group benefits when properly prioritized and managed.

Understanding Your Organization's Project Management Structure

It is essential to understand the organization that you will be working in. This section will help you understand the basic differences between organizations and how they perform and support project management. This will enable you to discuss these as you are being interviewed, not only making you look informed, but enabling you to determine what type of environment you are going to be working in.

There are three basic kinds of project organizations; program based, matrix based and project based. It is important to understand the differences between these structures as you seek out your next career to understand the politics, resourcing, climate, chain of command and informal "who's in charge" construct.

There are other instances where you may not recognize who you are working for within an organization that has project management. Many companies perform project management under other names. Still, other companies have no appreciation for any formal process. However, you may walk into a company that understands the essentials of project management, thus exploiting this organizational capability. Therefore, this varietal understanding drives the various organizational structures seen below.

Program-Based Organization

The first project management organization you may encounter is the program-based organization (Figure 3.2). Typically, this type of organization exists for production or integration purposes and is more often found in a DoD contract environment. You will find a program manager working under some kind of business unit director. He or she will be balancing the day-to-day health and financial fitness of the entire program, while working through problems that are occurring with personnel and the customer. The program manager may have an engineer lead and will have multiple projects or tasks with site leads reporting regularly.

The PMs may very well be technical leads themselves. Depending on the size of the projects, the PM may have a project coordinator on their staff to assist with scheduling and cost management. Resources should already be assigned to your project. You may be responsible for the hiring and firing of resources, but you will generally find that you have assigned resources to perform the work in your project.

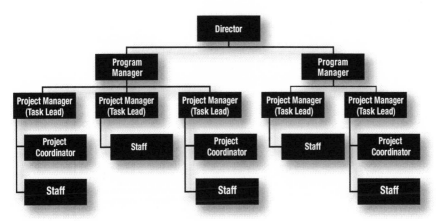

Figure 3.2 | Program Based Organization

Matrix-Based Organization

The Matrix-Based Organization (MBO) (Figure 3.3) will have functional or task leads working for a program manager. PMs receive resources from functional leads. No dedicated resources are provided to the PM. This is a very common type of organization in DoD and is a challenging environment for PMs. Rarely do you find dedicated support in this type of organization. Instead, you may have to "beg, borrow and steal" resources to assist you with your projects. Further, once you do get resources, they will be beholden to the functional leader rather than the PM, meaning they are often pulled off tasks at a moment's notice for other organizational challenges or issues. On a positive note, if a good project priority system, sound processes software tools such as MS project are utilized and adhered to, then this type of system not only works well for resource allocation and aligning skillsets appropriately, it also provides a more financially lucrative workforce. Finally, as depicted below, this organization may have a PMO. Because the PMO may appear in other organizations, a discussion of this office is provided at the end of this section.

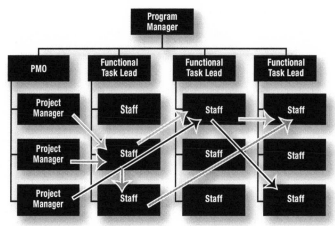

Figure 3.3 | Matrix-Based Organization

Project-Based Organization

The Project-Based Organization (PBO) (Figure 3.4) is more common in commercial environments and somewhat rare in the DoD environment. This type of organization has a PM with dedicated resources to the project. The PM has a high level of authority. He or she has the ability to use resources from inside and outside the organization, based on scope and money. The organizational focus is the project, schedule and cost. Resources are assigned for one purpose, the completion of the project. This project type is often used in construction and for the installation of infrastructure such as building wind generators and cell towers.

Figure 3.4 | Project-Based Organization

Project Management Office

The PMO is a much-needed discipline to facilitate portfolio management methodology. In Figure 3.3 of the MBO, the PMO entity is introduced. The PMO is becoming more prevalent and provides significant value through developing repeatable processes while standardizing outcomes, project analysis, and production of reports and metrics for management.

However, PMOs themselves are not a 'silver bullet' for project success. If not implemented correctly, it can be seen as a 'paper tiger' and a bureaucratic choke point. In 2012, the average age of the PMO when it was terminated was 4.1 years. Company reorganization, cost concerns, lack of executive support and corporate strategic alignment, perceived redundant work being performed elsewhere in the organization, and ineffectiveness are the most common reasons for terminating a PMO[7].

The degree of control and influence that a PMO manager has on projects depends on the type of PMO structure within the organization. The greater alignment of the PMO to the organizational culture and their strategic goals, the more responsive and credible the PMO will be[8].

Understanding Agile Project Management

As you transition into this great career field, you need to be aware of the growing popularity of Agile project management. Agile management's increasing usage over the past 15 years and has taken the project management field by storm and challenged how work should be completed, especially in a software or programming environment. Specific approaches of Agile known by many as Scrum, Kanban, SAFe, XP or Extreme Programming, share unique qualities of iterative development and continuous feedback during the project and/or software development lifecycle.

Today, the Agile approach is overwhelmingly used within software development centers. Agile software development uses various approaches where requirements and solutions evolve through collaborative effort of self-organizing and cross-functional teams and their customer(s) or end user(s).

It advocates adaptive planning, evolutionary development, early delivery, and continual improvement, and it encourages rapid and flexible response to changing requirements.

Some of the reasons for the Agile methodologies growing popularity is based upon the following:

- Faster delivery times of incremental product
- Continuous feedback
- Consistent ownership of work
- Rapid response to new issues
- Quality built into product
- Improved information sharing across the organization
- Customer involvement from the beginning and throughout the effort
- Work should be completed in short or iterative cycles called sprints
- Work is delivered through a group of people specifically and dedicated to the effort

In most cases, Agile is an iterative process and enables a flexible design model. Customers are committed to the process and involved throughout the whole Agile lifecycle, especially when end-goals and/or requirements are not well defined. Testing is of iterations or releases, and is typically performed concurrently with programming. The theory is that Agile teams are committed throughout the whole development process, leading to better cohesion and faster problem solving and development. Agile is very good in environments where the expectation is that software development planning will require frequent modifications to keep up customer requirement, market or technology evolution.

Comparing Traditional (Waterfall) Project Management to Agile

Agile is formal method of project management and is often compared to traditional or waterfall project management. This Agile process contrasts with the traditional approach to software development, a method where developers typically compile the needs and requirements of the users and then build the software all at once, with the completed project released at the very end of the project cycle. Agile will deliver frequent incremental releases after sprints or short established durations of time, so the customer can provide feedback and development team can validate and/or modify while moving on to the next increment.

Some organizations are looking to transition into more of a hybrid Agile approach that combines the best aspect of both Agile and Waterfall. The Project Management Institute (PMI) current Project Management Body of Knowledge® (PMBOK®) Guide is infused with Agile terms and philosophies. Included with the PMBOK® is the Agile Practice Guide, developed in collaboration between PMI and the Agile Alliance, specifically to help organizations understand and evaluate the use of Agile and hybrid Agile approaches.

As PMI® is recognized as the industry leader for traditional or waterfall project management, the Scrum Alliance (SA) is recognized for its leadership in Agile methodology and certification processes. These two organizations lead the world in traditional and agile certifications as seen in Appendix C.

The Agile Organization

Few true agile corporations exist. You will often find agile teams, projects and people, but for an organization to be completely agile, requires a tremendous mind shift; very few corporations have attempted it.

Three basic frameworks to making an agile organization work are:

Cross-functional teams: To appeal to the needs of their customers, teams need a good mix of skilled staff. Cross-functional teams are responsible for the delivery of a product or service from design to completion, dissimilar to traditional or matrix management structures. There should be no need to handover product development to other teams at a pre-determined stages.

Self-organizing teams: In agile, the responsibility and authority to create a functional, internal team structure by replacing, retraining, or re-organizing the team members as needed is a necessity. This situation arises when the customer's needs exceed the team's current capabilities. The team should then self-organize by moving or recruiting appropriately skilled staff.

Self-Management (or Empowerment): The largest challenge to developing an organization that is agile is the allowance of management to let go. Bureaucracy and management desire to ensure that team outcomes align with customer expectations and corporate strategy. Allowing the teams to self-manage and be accountable; with the authority to engage and deliver to the customers without undue interference is often a great of a challenge for management.

Even though there is tremendous variety, an organizational chart (Figure 3.5) is presented to assist in the basic understanding of the Agile Organization.

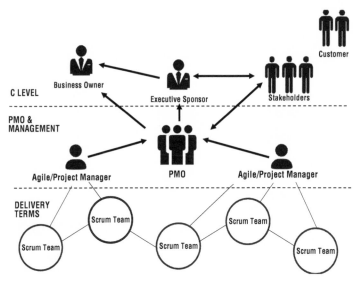

Figure 3.5 | Agile Organizational Chart

The Way Ahead

Now that you have a basic understanding of project management and organizational relationships, you need an understanding of the associated positions within this career field. With your skills and attributes, there are multiple insertion levels that lead to potential post transitional jobs for you. Applying your personal knowledge, with an understanding of positions and career paths, while taking the appropriate steps toward certification is instrumental to your success. This section will help firm up your way ahead within this exciting career field.

Career Path

Many future PMs transition into a project team and are assigned junior level responsibilities for one aspect of the project work. As experience is gained, they are assigned more tasks to manage, until they are ready to lead others in completing an entire project. Some PMs transition from primarily technical jobs, such as database administrator. Others initially find themselves creating, tracking, and updating the project schedule using a software program; reviewing documents, and writing reports. The desire to be more involved with the leadership, planning and pursuit of project management is a natural progression for many. There is not a singular project management career path. Instead, multiple paths are available allowing you to choose a path to the executive table, or to focus expertise within a specialized skill or product area. These specialty areas offer flexibility to increase expertise in a particular area you find interesting, evolving into Subject Matter Expert (SME) within many corporations. Thankfully, there are many options available to pursue, all offering a satisfying career in project management. The following diagram (Figure 3.6) and narrative depict typical project management positions. For those interested in focusing on a specialty area to become a Subject Matter Expert (SME) within project management, management options can range from quality, risk, scheduling, and agile, which are detailed later in this chapter. Included are some insights and descriptions to the expectations and skills to be performed and the title of associated certifications. Understand that this is not a singular career ladder that must be followed like a military rank system. You may skip or enter in at different levels depending on your project management experience and personal goals and ambitions. Further, you may find yourself stepping backwards due to personal occupational enjoyment, change in industry, location or salary.

Position Descriptions

The following section offers a description of positions within the project management career field as shown above. Not all positions and titles listed will be used in an organization. In fact, many will have modified names. Getting comfortable with the terminology and the requirements of the positions will enable you to approach each new opportunity with vigor and enthusiasm.

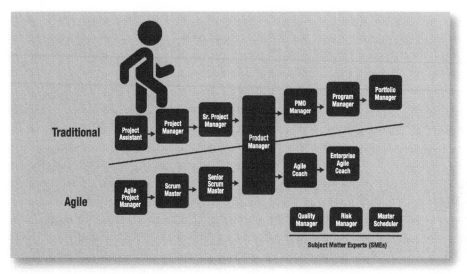

Figure 3.6 | Career Path Positions

Traditional Roles

Project Coordinator / Assistant

A Project Coordinator (PC) is an entry-level position that offers exposure to the work done by PMs. PCs work with the PM regularly to report progress, problems, and are usually assigned specific tasks to manage. This is normally an administrative position involving processing and paperwork. The PC will generate and distribute reports, keeping the project management team, owners, company staff, and others informed of a project progress. Other tasks such as scheduling meetings and assisting the management team with documentation are often given to the PC. Coordinators are not an alternative to a PM. PMI offers the Certified Associate project manager (CAPM®) certification, which is the most commonly associated certification with this position and will be discussed later in the chapter.

Project Manager

This is the person assigned by the performing organization to lead the team that is responsible for achieving project objectives. In this position, you may run a project yourself or lead a management team, delegating task management to assistants. PMs report to the "owner" of a project, whether that's a real estate developer, government agency, sponsor, or senior management. PMs oversee budget and schedule. Several project management certifications are discussed later.

Senior Project Manager

Many large organizations that tackle multiple projects at once, especially construction, IT and engineering companies, employ senior PMs. The senior PM supervises a company's various PMs, coordinating the allocation of company resources, approving costs, and working with management in deciding which projects take priority. Many senior PMs handle and work very complex and/or large projects. These projects might span multiple lines of business or be very visible to internal and external stakeholders. While similar in responsibility to PMs, senior PMs often tackle bigger projects and are asked to simultaneously advise and mentor younger PMs.

Product Manager

A product manager guides a team that is charged with a product line contribution to a business unit. This work extends from increasing the profitability of existing products to developing new products for the company. Product management requires a unique blend of business and technical savvy; a big-picture vision, and the drive to make that vision a reality. Time is spent to understand the problems and find innovative solutions for the broader market. Many organizations consider this position 'evangelistic', speaking to both internal and external groups on behalf of the product offering, occasionally working with the sales channel and key customers.

A product manager's key role is strategic, not tactical. Other organizational lines of business or divisions will support your strategic efforts;

you won't be supporting their tactical tasks. Association of International Product Marketing and Management (AIPMM) among other organizations, offer certifications in Certified Product Manager (CPM) and Certified Product Marketing Manager (CPMM).

PMO Manager

The PMO manager oversees the PMO process implementation and ensures that information concerning content (e.g., deliverables, risks, and issues) passes to and from sponsors. Generally, the PMO manager is a seasoned PM with many years of experience.

The PMO manager's focus involves improving the consistency, predictability and efficiency of the organization's project delivery capability. The PMO manager provides leadership in best practices and is highly customer-focused. They ensure the operational issues of the PMO are managed, focusing on the project interface with project leaders and teams, technology and interface issues. Oversight from a PMO manager can include monitoring profit and cost sheets, utilizing earned value management (EVM), reports on active projects, and portfolios. PMO managers regularly brief senior leadership on a variety of topics including strategic alignment of projects, pipeline projects and other portfolio management issues in the absence of a portfolio manager.

Program Manager

The program manager has oversight of the purpose and status of all projects in a program. This oversight ensures that overall program goals are likely to be met, through a decision-making capacity that cannot be achieved at a project level. Typically in a program, there is a need to identify and manage cross-project dependencies. The PMO may not have sufficient insight of the risk, issues, requirements, design or solution to accurately brief senior leadership. The program manager is well suited to provide this insight by actively seeking out such information from the PMs and making leadership corrections to ensure project success. The program manager needs to manage and achieve overall program goals and maximize benefits realized by the aggregate of projects within the program. Recognizing the advanced experience and skills of program managers, PMI offers the program management Professional (PgMP®) certification.

Portfolio Manager

The management issues with project-oriented portfolio management can be judged by criteria such as return on investment (ROI), strategic alignment, maintenance savings, and suitability of resulting solutions including the relative value of new investments to replace outdated or out-of-warranty items.

Benefits of using portfolio management include central oversight of budget, risk management, strategic alignment of IT investments, with demand and investment management as well as standardization of investment procedure, rules and plans. Most essential to portfolio managers is demonstrating how they utilize projects/programs to balance the prioritization of projects between risk and return. Additionally, portfolio managers oversee the full life-cycle of program/project efforts from pipeline, to active project, to sustainment and retirement.

As of 2014, PMI offers the Portfolio Management Professional (PfMP®) certification.

Agile Roles

With the goal focused on a single product/application, there is a team approach for accomplishing incremental products using Agile. Not all agile organizations have all positions. Responsibilities vary from organization and are sometimes shared. A typical Agile team structure consists of the following positions:

Development or Scrum Team

This is the group doing the actual developing, and is typically made up of engineers, designers, architects and testers. Often, the team self-manages rather than being managed by a Project Manager.

Agile Manager

The agile manager is responsible for resourcing, planning, leading, organizing, and motivating agile project teams to achieve high level performance and quality throughout the project lifecycle. In performing this role, the agile manager may be expected to use knowledge and experience to blend traditional project management principles and practices with an agile development approach to provide the right balance of agility and predictability.

Scrum Master

This dual role of coach and gatekeeper establishes responsibility for following the Agile framework, providing guidance and education, and removing impediments and distractions. They are a facilitator that builds a self-organization team. Using servant leadership, they help empower the team while protecting them from external disturbance.

Senior Scrum Master

They are the subject matter experts for the given project. They can be a member of the customer organization or responsible for the delivery of the product to the customer. Either way, the Senior Scrum Master keeps track of the projects stakeholders' expectations; defining and gathering the required tools and resources. In addition, the Senior Scrum Master communicates their vision to the team in order to set priorities.

Agile Coach

An Agile Coach works with multiple teams, executives, and other groups as opposed to a Scrum Master who works with a single team. The Agile Coach ensures Scrum process and rules are followed, enabling the adoption and improvement of agile methodologies.

An Agile Coach role is part trainer and part consultant, who continues training team members after the formal classes. They are a change agent; someone who is both motivating change and making it happen.

This position requires a requires a breadth of knowledge on leadership, business, processes and technology, mixed with skills in facilitation, mentoring, advising.

The instrumental position of Agile Coach is a prominent role on the Agile career path. These folks are well beyond the basic knowledge of Scrum and Product owner, as they refine foundational practices of Agile, Lean, and Design Thinking for the organization.

Enterprise Agile Coach

As the title denotes, an Enterprise Agile coach works at the enterprise level. While the underlying skills of coaching are similar to that of an Agile coach, an enterprise Agile coach has to possess knowledge of organizational design, enterprise change management, and executive leadership coaching. An Enterprise Agile coach is concerned with helping to change the overall structure of the company through facilitating Agile principles, advocating Agile practices, managing organizational and culture change, and introduces enterprise-level Agile methodologies. Aaron Kopel of Project Brilliant, states the Enterprise Agile Coach is an expert, with knowledge and understanding of enterprise Agile frameworks like Scaled Agile Framework (SAFe), Large-scale Scrum (LeSS) or Disciplined Agile Delivery (DaD).

Specialty Roles

Master Scheduler (SME)

For large projects or programs, a master scheduler runs the project scheduling software, inputting information supplied by the management team and updating files as needed. This is a technical position that involves a great deal of scheduling, typically with software application management and little actual project management. This position would manage many schedules and work with multiple PMs and teams to derive standards for work schedules and manage resources using a commercially available software scheduling tool like

Microsoft Project, ZOHO Projects, FastTrack Schedule 9, Primavera P6, or @task. A strong knowledge or certification of a scheduling software tool is likely required or, at a minimum, highly desirable. The DoD has recognized the importance of a master scheduler through guidebooks, as referenced in previous sections of this chapter. If you pursue this functional area, you may desire to become credentialed with the PMI-SP® (Scheduling Professional) certification or gain a tool specific certification such as Microsoft Project. Both of these are discussed in the credentialing section later in this chapter.

Quality Manager (SME)

Quality manager duties include oversight and review, data accuracy and reporting, as well as interacting with auditors for regulatory compliance. Other functions include coordinating and facilitating various projects to ensure that Quality Improvement (QI) goals and objectives are accomplished through judicious and efficient use of resources. In other words, you must manage all company-wide, quality policies, procedures, processes, programs, and practices, to assure the company continuous conformance with appropriate standards and regulations. In a smaller company, you may also be the document control manager, quality auditor, and process improvement specialist. A quality manager should have an understanding of Lean Six Sigma and the statistical measurement of data to include such areas as: design of experiments, Define-Measure-Analyze-Improve-Control (DMAIC), statistical process control, root cause analysis, cause and effect diagrams and value stream mapping. Certifications in areas such as

American Society for Quality (ASQ) offers certifications in quality for: Manager, Auditor, and Technician at:
asq.org

International Association for Six Sigma (IASSC) offers universal standards testing at:
iassc.org

IEEE offers an array of quality based standards at:
iso.org

quality and Six Sigma are advisable. Additionally, the Institute of Electrical and Electronics Engineers (IEEE) is entering multiple project manage00ment credential markets, including the International Organization for Standardization (ISO) 10006:2003, Quality Management systems – Guidelines for Quality Management in projects, and ISO 10007:2003, Quality Management systems – Guidelines for Configuration Management.

Risk Manager (SME)

Risk management is a natural follow on career for some in the project management field. Typically, the risk manager advises organizations on any potential risks to profitability. This position studies probability and severity of potential risks, both positive and negative. Risk managers identify and assess threats, put mitigation plans in place for potential risks and decide how to avoid, reduce or transfer risks.

Risk managers are responsible for managing the risk to the organization, its employees, customers, reputation, assets and interests of stakeholders. They may work in a variety of sectors and may specialize in a number of areas. These areas may include enterprise risk, corporate governance, regulatory and operational risk, business continuity, information and security risk, technology risk, and market and credit risk. PMI's Risk Management Professional (PMI-RMP®) certification, the Institute for Risk Auditors' Certification in Risk Management Assurance (CRMA) certification, and the IEEE ISO 31000:2009 certification are well respected certifications in Risk Management.

Hedging Your Bet – Certification

Which Project Certification is right?
pmexam.com/
pmi-certification/

The Project Management Industry has grown dramatically world wide. Not surprisingly, within this important career field, there has been a massive proliferation of certifications. Thirteen major organizations provide certifications around the world in support this industry. Appendix C provides the top ranking organizations from both the US Defense and commercial industries. Using this appendix, you can learn more about the variety of certification authorities. However, as the premier certification authority, this chapter focuses primarily on the PMI(R) certification and exam process.

There are multiple avenues for certification. You may desire a commercial certification in project management through an organization like PMI, or a tool specific certification through a vendor like Microsoft. Some certifications are less rigid with eligibility requirements, cost, and exam questions. If you are going to remain in the government sector, you may desire or be required to obtain a government certification through the Defense Acquisition University (DAU). This section will enhance your knowledge of these certification paths.

Commercial Certifications

If you decide to work as a contractor or move toward commercial industry and desire to manage projects, enhance your expertise and expand your career options, you should obtain an industry-recognized certification. A commercially recognized project management certification validates to employers that you have the knowledge, experience and education to effectively lead or contribute to project team success.

Project-Road.com
Inexpensive on-line Training for Military & Veterans

Additionally, certification is the fastest route to a higher salary and more opportunities for growth and hiring. For example, those who have held the PMP credential for two to four years earn, an estimated 20% more than their non-credentialed colleagues who have similar experience.[9] A more in depth discussion on salary can be found in Chapter Four.

Over the years, project management certifications have become more of a requirement than just a desirable accomplishment. Project management certification has quickly become the prerequisite to get your foot into a career door. Regardless, both professional and financial rewards will follow with certifications.

International Certifications

Professional certification in project management is available through many credentialing bodies worldwide. You may want to consider your desired location of employment prior to obtaining your certification. For example, ISO has joined forces with PMI to create ISO 21500 as the first in a planned family of project management standards. IEEE Standards Association has adopted the PMBOK®. The International Project Management Association (IPMA) offers similar certifications to PMI including: Project Director, Senior Project Manager, Project Manager, and Project Manager Associate. The American Academy of Certified Project Managers (AAPM) also offers such certifications as the Certified International Project Manager (CIPM®) and Master Project Manager®.

Project + Certification

Project+ from CompTIA is another method for certification. CompTIA states that the Project+ certification is vendor neutral, cost-effective and can be earned in a reasonable period of time. Further, CompTIA states that the Project+ certification validates PMs and team members have the classic project management skills to help those complete projects on time and within budget. The Project+ exam is a 100-question test covering topics of project initiation, planning, execution, acceptance, support and closure. CompTIA allows 90 minutes for the examination.[10]

Tool Specific Certification

If you are interested in a project control or scheduler position, then you may desire to obtain a tool specific certification. For example, Microsoft offers a series of certifications based upon their MS-project management software, including the enterprise level. Microsoft offers designation as a Microsoft Certified Technology Specialist (MCTS) and other certifications in Microsoft Office Project 2007, 2010, and

Microsoft Project Management certifications
https://study.com/ microsoft_project_ management_ certification.html
Training for Military & Veterans

2013. PMs must pass a written examination issued by Microsoft in order to earn their MCTS certification. The exam measures knowledge of all major controls and functions of Microsoft Project, including creating project templates, developing budgets and schedules, delegating tasks and resources, and tracking and analyzing project success.

PMI® Certification

The Project Management Institute offers a comprehensive certification program for project practitioners of all education and skill levels. There are currently nine credentials available that are rigorously developed, globally accredited and easily transferable across borders and industries.

PMI Certifications:
pmi.org/Certifications/types

PMIs cornerstone and most revered credential is the PMP, recognized globally. Currently, PMI offers the following credentials:

- CAPM® (Certified Associate Project Management)
- PMP® (Project Management Professional)
- PgMP® (Program Management Professional)
- PfMP® (Portfolio Management Professional)
- PMI-RMP® (Risk Management Professional)
- PMI-SP® (Scheduling Professional)
- PMI-ACP® (Agile Certified Practitioner)
- PMI-PBA® (PMI Professional in Business Analysis)

Requirements

The detailed requirements and essential tools for project management certification can be found at www.pmi.org. This web site will not only provide all the information and data you need to make the decision on which certification to pursue, but will also step you through the process. The most commonly requested and obtained PMI certifications from the list above are CAPM®, PMP®, ACP, and PgMP®. Figure 3.7 is a comparative list of eligibility requirements for the three major certifications, with regard to education and experience. It is essential to apply for the correct certification, as all are desirable, but have very different requirements.

Educational Background	CAPM® Project Experience	PMP® Project Experience	PgMP® Project Experience	ACP® Project Experience
High school diploma, associate's degree, or global equivalent	At least 1 year (1,500) hours of project experience	Minimum 5 years (7,500) hours of non-overlapping project management experience	6,000 hours of non-overlapping project management experience **PLUS** 7 years (10,500) hours of program management experience*	2,000 hours general project experience** (** a PMP® or PgMP® cert will satisfy requirement) **PLUS** 1,500 hours agile project or methodology experience
		OR	**OR**	
Bachelor's degree, global equivalent or higher degree		Minimum 3 years (4,500) hours of non-overlapping project management experience	6,000 hours of non-overlapping project management experience **PLUS** at least 6,000 hours of **program** management experience*	
OR	**OR**	**AND**		**AND**
Training	23 hours education	35 hours education Or CAPM® cert.	—	21 hours agile training / education

Figure 3.7 | CAPM®, PMP®, and PgMP® Credential Eligibility Requirements

Certified Associate in Project Management (CAPM®)

The CAPM® recognizes a demonstrated understanding of the fundamental knowledge, terminology and processes of effective project management. Any member of a project team who is lacking in experience for full PMP certification and provides subject matter expertise (e.g., marketing, customer care, processing, and fulfillment) should work toward this certification.

Project Management Professional (PMP®)

The PMP®, which is the anchor certification for PMI, recognizes demonstrated experience, skill and performance in leading and directing projects. The PMP® certification is increasingly being sought after as a required certification for jobs. The PMP® is a world-wide, recognized certification with over 600,000 current PMP® holders, proving the argument that U.S. project management jobs are becoming increasingly more difficult to obtain without the PMP® certification.

Program Management Professional (PgMP®)

The PgMP® credential recognizes demonstrated experience, skill and performance in the oversight of multiple, related projects that are aligned with organizational objectives. Those who manage programs containing complex activities spanning functions, organizations, geographic regions and cultures should apply for this credential.

As you mature in your project management skills, or if you have already had programmatic experience, you may wish to pursue a program management certification (PgMP®). The PgMP® exam tests the ability, knowledge and experience of program management. The exam is largely experiential and factual knowledge should already be in your back pocket.

The PgMP® application includes answering five domain questions, presenting your real-world knowledge and experience.[11] You will need to understand and be able to defend the benefits measured throughout the programs and portfolios you lead. These exams are about experience; understanding terms, inputs, outputs, and tools.

Agile Certified Professional (ACP)

If you work or plan on working with agile teams, the PMI-ACP may be the correct choice for you. Compared with other agile certifications based solely on training and exams, the PMI-ACP is evidence of your real-world, hands-on experience and skill. Therefore, as shown in table 3.7 above, you will need to demonstrate your personal experience in Agile, during the application process.

Application

To obtain the PMP® credential, applicants must first satisfy assessment requirements in which you report acquired project management education and experience. By agreeing to a code of ethics and paying examination fees, you study and pass the PMP® certification examination. We will talk about each of these independently.

The PMP®, like most technical certifications, requires experience. Like a race car driver, a PM must have seat time to be successful. Seat time means bringing experience to the table, so that your credential knowledge enhances your current capabilities. Professional race car drivers understand road conditions and racing experience teaches what it is like to actually feel the rubber against the road and how a car handles on different surfaces. Your time in the military has given you this seat time. You have been a planner and executer on many projects. It is essential that you understand and believe you have this experience, even though you approach this from a different career field. You will be asked for your seat time when you go through the assessment process for your certification and at any interview.

The challenge for most during the assessment is getting the 7500 hours (4500 if you have a Bachelor's Degree) documented onto the Certification Application. This can be a challenge if you do not understand how your military experience relates to the PMI process groups. To assist in this endeavor, a "Rosetta Stone" can be found in Appendix B. This tool relates military planning processes from each service to process groups. This should not only help align your thoughts for the application, but can also be used to assist in relating your military experiences to your civilian interviewer or hiring manager.

Code of Ethics

You will be asked to comply with a code of ethics during the application process. PMI states "...the Code of Ethics and Professional Conduct describes the expectations that we have of ourselves and our fellow practitioners in the global project management community. It articulates the ideals to which we aspire as well as the behaviors that are mandatory in our professional and volunteer roles."[12]

Study and Exam

As with most certifications, there are a host of on-line and classroom training typically called prep classes which prepare you for taking the exam. In addition to the recommended reading of standard and best practices, most training institutes will review the following areas that will be found on the test during a prep class:

- Process
- Methodology
- Domains or Knowledge Areas
- Terminology
- Exam questions (factual, and scenario based)
- Exam types (multiple choice)
- General preparation and application assistance

Some boot camps are a good method in learning how to pass the test, but still require considerable study time outside the class. Some boot camps even offer guarantees to passing the exam, if you pass their course. On the downside, these are very expensive should you have to pay for them yourself.

Fortunately for you as a transitioning service member, you now have many free and low cost options available. Further, a significant amount of training is available to you before you leave the service. It is recommended that you explore the different options and take the available online courses. Additionally, funds for training and testing reimbursement are available to you after you leave the service from the Veterans Administration and G.I. Bill. Regardless, take advantage of every opportunity for education as soon as you can.

Military Certification Resource Options

Army

Through the Army Credentialing Opportunities Online (COOL) program, enlisted soldiers can learn about resources to receive reimbursement and training for the Project Management Professional certification. The exam has been approved for payment through the G.I. Bill. The COOL Website has state-of-the-art, computer-based project management training available, free to the army workforce.

Navy and Marine Corps

Interestingly, the Navy COOL Website has similar capabilities as the Army site, with the exception of the free on-line computer training capability.

Air Force

At the Air Force Institute of Technology, students taking the FAM 103 course will spend a week studying the basics of project management skills based on the Project Management Body of Knowledge from the Project Management Institute.

MILITARY COOL PROJECT TRAINING & CERTIFICATION

ARMY: cool.army.mil
NAVY: cool.navy.mil
AIR FORCE: https://afvec.langley.af.mil/afvec/Public/COOL/Default.aspx

No Cost Training - Veterans

For those in transition, there are classes you may take through the Institute for Veteran and Military Families (IVMF). The classes are at NO COST to the veteran, from Syracuse University. Options include CAPM® and PMP® through either a professional track or an independent study track.

Government Certification

For those desiring to stay in the DoD acquisition career field as a civil servant, often the DAU certification process is an appropriate method for job security and promotion. Remember, anyone in the acquisition career field can take the training, but only civil servants and active duty military can get the certification. The Defense Acquisition Workforce Improvement Act (DAWIA) required the DoD to establish a process through which persons in the acquisition workforce would be recognized as having achieved professional status. Certification is the procedure through which a military service or DoD Component determines that an employee meets the education, training, and experience standards required for a career level in any acquisition, technology, and logistics career field."[13]

Certifications are only available for DoD civilian employees, military and civilians assigned to an acquisition coded position and select military officers whose career development will include assignment to acquisition-coded positions. Even though

DAU Courses:
dau.mil

certification is not a qualification requirement for employment within the DoD, job announcements will view this certification as a "quality ranking factor" not a "qualification factor". Therefore, all DoD personnel filling acquisition positions have 24 months to achieve the certification standards (career field/path and level) assigned to the position.

DAU CAREER FIELD CERTIFICATION FUNCTIONAL AREAS

Auditing	Information Technology
Business – Cost Estimating	Life Cycle Logistics
Business – Financial Management	Program Management
Contracting	Production, Quality and Manufacturing
Engineering	Purchasing
Facilities Engineering	Science and Technology Manager
Industrial/Contract Property Management	Test and Evaluation

Figure 3.8 | DAU Career Field Certification Functional Areas

In addition to the Level I, II and III, career field guides are given on the DAU site for the most current career field certification standards required of Defense Acquisition Workforce in accordance with the acquisition position. As of the date of this book's publication, Figure 3.8 shows the career field certifications currently available through DAU.[14]

For example, if you want to go the program management route with DAU, you would need to qualify at Level I, II, or III, depending on your position. You do not necessarily have to qualify at each level in order, but Level III would require prerequisites from the lower level certifications. Each requirement for each acquisition career field is specified at the DAU Website. By way of example, Figure 3.9 shows the requirements for DAWIA certification of Level I in the program management career field.

The silver lining for government certification is two-fold. First, this is high quality, government specific, on-line training available to you. The second is that this training is available free of charge. If you go the civil service route, this training is absolutely essential and will propel your career while significantly enhancing your knowledge and skills.

CORE CERTIFICATION STANDARDS (REQUIRED FOR DAWIA CERTIFICATION)

Acquisition Training	ACQ 101 Fundamentals of Systems Acquisition Management
Functional Training	SYS 101 Fundamentals of Systems Planning, Research, Development, and Engineering
	CLB 007 Cost Analysis
	CLV 016 Introduction to Earned Value Management
Education	Formal education not required for certification
Experience	1 year of acquisition experience with cost, schedule, and performance responsibilities

Figure 3.9 | Core Certification Standards

Comparing Government and Commercial Project Management Certifications

For those interested in a comparison between commercial project management certifications and government-based project management certifications, few alignments exist. The matrix below offers comparison of three major groups of certifications available to both transitioning and military personnel: PMI, DAU DAWIA and DAU Federal Acquisition Certification (FAC).

Using the matrix below, the PMI certifications focus on the Project Management Body of Knowledge, for all types of projects and anyone who has the prerequisite experience to apply. If you are heading to the commercial sector, then PMI certification is appropriate.

However, if you are considering staying in the government or DoD sector, you may want to take a close look at the two government credentials focusing on the acquisition process, policy and its regulations. These are very specific, credentials for those interested in remaining in DoD acquisition. While the training is available to any employee in the DoD sector, neither government credential is available once you leave the military unless you become a civil servant. There are many other credentialing bodies offering certifications. Appendix C shows certifications that are available now. Understanding and selecting the appropriate credential is extremely important to your preparation for transition. Therefore, study the nuances of each certification as they apply to your interests and career path goals and add this credentialing process to your transition plan and Personal Strategic Roadmap.

Military to Project Management Lexicon

Communication is key to landing the right job. In order to land the right job, you must be able to translate what you have done as a Military PM into commercial project management words.

The World English Dictionary defines the noun 'lexicon' as a list of terms relating to a particular subject; the vocabulary of a language or individual. Appendix A provides a lexicon to assist in translating familiar military terms to their commercial equivalent. As mentioned in chapter two, the value is multifaceted. First, you can use these during resume writing to translate military terminology with commercial terminology. The second major benefit is for your understanding of terminology during the interview process, enabling you to use commercial terminology when describing your military project efforts.

For simplicity and use of this table in Appendix A, we have listed only the most common commercial terms. This list is merely an example of the multitude of terms and concepts that must be translated from the military to the commercial vernacular. Once you get comfortable with the wording translation, you will then be able to think of your own. To assist others in translation of their experience and military vernacular, we would love to hear from you and have you share your own word translations on the GR8militaryPM.com website.

For a larger list of lexicon translations, visit:
GR8MilitaryPM.com

Assessment #4 *(Skills)*

Figure 3.10 is the fourth assessment in the book and explores your personal preparedness for the career field of project management. You may answer the assessment questions here. When you are ready to analyze them, refer to Chapter Five. You can also utilize the companion guide to this book, available for download and print at www.gr8militarypm.com. Read each question and choose the correct answer for your current situation.

4: SKILLS ASSESSMENT	Strongly Disagree	Disagree	Neither Agree OR Disagree	Agree	Strongly Agree
I am interested in project management as a future career.					
I have earned a project management certification.					
I have performed project management related tasks in the past.					
I have led operations and planning efforts in the past.					
I have created training schedules or plans.					
I have reviewed different types of PM certification and analyzed the best certification for my situation.					
I enjoy leading groups and organizations.					
I have planned exercise or operations in the military.					
I have controlled, changed and adjusted mission, projects or training schedules.					
I desire to get certified as a project manager prior to leaving the service.					

Figure 3.10 | Skills Assessment

Summary

Once comfortable with the basics, project management knowledge will place you at a competitive advantage. You can inquire and ask questions at the end of an interview such as how the company views different positions; how risk adverse the company is; how mature their documentation processes are; what tools are used; and what career path options are open to someone starting in your position and what criteria is used to measure and advance.

The choice to prepare yourself to meet your organization's needs and to enjoy the career benefits of being properly prepared is yours to make. We encourage you to continue your education and learn project management as a profession to gain an awareness that transcends job titles, careers, and industries. Just as the story below indicates, many have transitioned before you into this exciting career field and you will too. The real-world, best-practice tools and techniques that you successfully use to provide organizational leadership and gain a personal competitive advantage will be recognized for many years to come!

Terry Wright
Determined to Succeed

Terry Wright graduated from high school in 1983 during a tough unemployment period in Indiana. He came from a difficult environment where a high school education was considered success. Terry knew he needed college, but had no money, credit or guidance. He leveraged the Indiana Army National Guard's student loan repayment program, worked two part-time jobs and obtained an Associate Degree in Electronics Engineering Technology. After being called up during the first Gulf War as an electronics technician, he moved to Indianapolis as a field engineer, installing and servicing computer based networks using Novell NetWare. As an outgrowth of his engineering capability, he managed projects in a paperless medical record work flow system in hospitals, learning project management on the fly.

Ten years later, Terry eventually was promoted several times within the company, ultimately becoming the Senior Director. He attended night school and studied software and database design. During this period, Terry remained active with the Army National Guard with several highly successful rotations to the Joint Readiness Training Center (JRTC) with the 101st Airborne Divisions, and the 5th Special Forces Group. He was personally contacted by the Ohio Air National Guard 251st Combat Communications Group (CCG) and recruited to jump services to help with the Air Force Tactical Communications. On 9/11, Terry was called up along with elements of his group for 24 months in support of the Afghanistan war. He began the tour as a network defense specialist and after a couple months was asked to finish a pilot project replacing grease pencils and acetate with an online, web-based system named Theater Aerospace Systems Reporting (TASR). Four months after returning from the Afghanistan tour, Terry received a call to return for another 12 months in support of the Iraq War. During this tour he managed large IT projects, replacing tactical communication systems at forward deployed locations with full scale Non-secure Internet Protocol Router Network (NIPRNet) and Secret Internet Protocol Router Network (SIPRNet).

Terry has no regrets about his active duty service, but there was a price. After returning from three years of activation, he found that he had lost his senior management job, had no professional network to utilize, nor adequate education to promote himself. Further, he was part of an undesirable military community due to the risk of follow-on activations. He now painfully understood the need for greater education. No longer was there "...a willingness to work hard to do most anything" philosophy to provide the security needed. He knew he would have to obtain education and certification. He landed a 90-day project management assignment in Sarasota, Florida formally scoping and planning a derailed IT paperless workflow infrastructure project. He found the environment to be brutal; managing 24 subordinate PMs in an atmosphere where degrees and certifications were literally worn on nametags like badges of honor. If you were not certified, every decision was questioned and your opinions were baseless. This is where Terry became painfully aware of the importance of education and certification and decided that he must pursue both.

Terry received an unsolicited call from a recruiter looking for a technical PM to work for the Defense Intelligence Agency (DIA) in Tampa, Florida. Within weeks of starting the job, he re-enrolled in college (Saint Leo University) and attended for the next three years to complete a Masters of Business Degree. Terry also completed CompTIA Project+ Certification, to shore up gaps in his education and make himself more secure on paper. Terry took advantage of ITIL training while at DIA, taking classes that had been dropped by others at the last minute then studying and passing the tests.

Terry was subsequently hired to work with the PMO at United States Central Command (USCENTCOM) managing an array of IT projects to include a massive 5,000 desk top replacement project. Just before the end of the contract and knowing he would have to move on, Terry accepted the lead of a struggling integration facility team. Terry quickly made some staffing changes, laid out a data center plan, launched its execution, developed a detailed team charter and passed the baton to the new contractor. Terry was offered a position at the acquisition center for United States Special Operations Command (USSOCOM) where he performed program IT support, project management and system engineering work. Utilizing much of what he was learning in his MBA program, Terry spent a lot of time developing return on investment (ROI) analysis, solution briefings and planning. Still feeling the need to have a better dossier, he studied and passed the PMP exam.

Having to once again slide into a new contract to survive as a DoD contractor, Terry found himself managing the relocation of 300 personnel to a new updated facility. Shortly after closing this successful project, he was offered a position with another company as a key member providing overall performance management of a Government contract. During this time, he built an enterprise PMO for the management of multiple globally dispersed components. With his two degrees, multiple certifications, and loads of experience, Terry was sought out by a company to become their deputy program manager, with the objective of transitioning his organization to the business processes he had helped to establish for the USSOCOM information technology contract. Once again, Terry began transitioning, stabilization and right-sizing the organization by placing personnel in correct positions and weeding out those who could not fulfill a role within the team, tasks he had previously performed many times before.

Terry continues to better himself in education, certification and experience, utilizing the G.I. Bill and all available company financial assistance. While working in an environment early in his career where he found the organization discriminating against non-educated and certified personnel, Terry drove himself to churn through multiple degrees and certifications so he would never have to deal with that challenge again. Terry never wanted his work, plans or management decisions to be challenged by the unscrupulous saying, "He doesn't have the education or certifications to work here!" Today, Terry claims the "most significant and career boosting certification he has ever obtained is clearly the PMP."

The Market Place

TREMENDOUS OPPORTUNITIES ABOUND IN THE COMMERCIAL AND PUBLIC SECTORS. The challenge is understanding and making an informed decision about where to conduct your job search. This very important decision needs to incorporate your comfort levels with risk, job satisfaction, security and growth. Learning about your desires as they relate to market place characteristics, will give you a distinct advantage in your job search decision.

You may have already settled on a target job market. However, if you are unsure, look to this chapter to provide you with the tools to evaluate the pros and cons of your target market place.

> **"Opportunities multiply as they are seized."**
>
> Sun Tzu 孫子
> *The Art of War*

Some transitioning personnel believe they will step into a great paying and interesting job for the rest of their life, immediately after leaving the service. However, this is not typical. Most of us change jobs, companies, and career fields many times. Learning the advantages and disadvantages of multiple transitions can better prepare you and your family.

Opportunities after the military service fall into roughly four sectors. Three of these sectors are the focus of this chapter; civil service, government contracting, and commercial market place. For those that enjoy risk and working independently, entrepreneurship is a fourth option. There is a wealth of knowledge readily available on the entrepreneurship market. Entrepreneurship is not a focus as it is beyond the scope and objective of this book.

Each market place is explored with regard to environment, opportunity, pay, benefits and career path as they relate to your interest and desires. Options and insights are offered so that you can weigh and consider all facets that impact you the most, from work/life balance to job benefits.

After looking at each sector, the market places are compared within the framework described above. A marketplace assessment is presented to further assist in identifying key factors while determining the best fit for you and your next position. As you read this chapter, note that the terms public sector, government, and civil service are all used interchangeably. Likewise, private sector, commercial company, and corporation are terms used in lieu of commercial market place. DoD Contracting is considered a hybrid to these distinct sectors.

Civil Service Market Place

The federal government is the largest employer in the nation, hiring nearly 300,000 new employees every year. There are many government departments and agencies. All have many differences, from culture, professional opportunity, and employee satisfaction, and in some cases, pay scales.[1] Generally, civil service provides a tremendous opportunity for those desiring a stable work environment, great benefits and good pay. The reality is that people do not take civil service positions to get wealthy. In general, gov-

Federal benefits
usa.gov/benefits-for-federal-employees

ernment workers want to use their skills and make a difference. Therefore, many choose civil service for these reasons, along with a growing number of transitioning military.

"Most candidates interested in working for the government fully understand three clear benefits," said Evan Lesser, co-founder and director of ClearanceJobs.com, a secure website designed to match security-cleared job candidates with top defense industry employers. "First, is the issue of job security. Compared to contractors, Federal agencies are less subject to budget funding shortfalls and cancelled or re-bid contracts. Second, job seekers see a more structured promotion ladder. And third, working for the nation's largest employer means excellent health and retirement benefits."[2] If you are unaware, workers in commercial firms are three times more likely to be fired, compared to federal employees. Civil service positions are generally more stable. This is comforting if stability is one of your most compelling decision factors.

Environment

The Partnership for Public Service (PPS), in concert with the audit and financial professional services firm Deloitte, annually publishes the *"The Best Places to Work in the Federal Government"*. This cross agency assessment provides civil servant's opinions on workplace issues ranging from leadership, work-life balance, pay and personal ability for innovation.

John Palguta, PPS Vice President of Policy, stated "The reason people go to work for the government is because they want to do something meaningful and make a difference. Civil servants want to make good use of their skills and be engaged in mission accomplishment." The PPS assessment demonstrates civil servant personal job satisfaction and overall organization satisfaction.[3] An important factor making up organization satisfaction is pay. The last couple of years have been difficult for civil servant salary increases. Not surprisingly, recent reports show a significant

Federal workplace survey:
bestplacestowork.org/
rankings/overall/large

categorical drop in satisfaction of federal pay, due to the political and economic environment. Potentially due to fiscal concerns, there was also a decline in training and development opportunities, and rewards and advancement.

Additionally, assessment results are broken into federal agency size categories. Not surprisingly, the Departments of Navy, Air Force and Army are all listed and considered large agencies with 15,000 or more employees. Interestingly, for the civil servants interviewed, National Aeronautics and Space Administration finished on top with the highest satisfaction, and the Department of Homeland Security finished last. Figure 4.1 provides statistical results in overall job satisfaction for all federal large agencies. No sector receives a perfect score of 100, but the higher the score, indicates greater personal job satisfaction within that agency.

RANK	LARGE AGENCY (15,000 OR MORE EMPLOYEES)	SCORE
1	National Aeronautics and Space Administration	81.2
2	Department of Health and Human Services	70.9
3	Department of Commerce	70.3
4	Department of Transportation	67.7
5	Intelligence Community	66.3
6	Department of Veterans Affairs	64.2
7	Department of the Navy	63.2
7	Office of the Secretary of Defense, Joint Staff, Defense Agencies, and Department of Defense Field Activities	63.2
9	Department of the Interior	62.8
10	Department of Justice	62.6
11	Department of the Army	62.4
12	Social Security Administration	61.9
13	Department of the Treasury	61.3
14	Department of State	60.7
15	Department of the Air Force	60.4
16	Department of Agriculture	59.0
17	Department of Homeland Security	53.1

Figure 4.1 | Statistical Results for Job Satisfaction – Large Agency[4]

Opportunity

Generally, civil service positions provide tremendous opportunities for military members in transition. The federal government gives you an advantage due to your veteran status. Having served in a war, having a military connected disability or having served on active duty all give you

Civil Service Job Site:
USAJOBS.GOV

an advantage and put you in different competitive categories. Therefore, your military service provides a significant benefit when competing for high quality civil-service positions.

When applying for civil service positions, you need to understand how the job announcement enables or precludes your advantageous veteran status. In many civil service applications, veteran status is awarded extra 'points' when identified by the applicant. You may be eligible to compete under one or more categories designed for veterans such as: Veterans' Recruitment Appointment (VRA), 30 Percent or More Disabled Veterans, or Veterans Employment Opportunities Act of 1998 (VEOA). These special hiring authorities for veterans give you a significant advantage if you are qualified. Figure 4.2 summarizes these hiring authorities for veterans:

Remember, your competition when applying for these positions are current federal employees with status and other United States citizens. Therefore, understanding your veteran eligibility is critical. Also, be aware that your eligibility does not make you qualified for the position. You may be eligible under a special hiring authority, but you may not be qualified based on your experience or education.

The difference between eligibility and qualifications can be summed up as follows. Qualification is based solely on your knowledge, skills, and abilities (KSA's), and education, as discussed in chapters two and three. Eligibility is meeting one or more criteria such as disabled veteran. A recent dimension in determining qualification for a job is the use of self-assessments, which are now becoming more of a standard than the exception. A series of questions are asked

AUTHORITY	PROVISION	WHO IT APPLIES TO
VRA	VRA allows appointment of eligible Veterans up to the GS-11 or equivalent grade level.	• Disabled Veterans • Veterans who served on active duty in the Armed Forces during a war declared by Congress, or in a campaign or expedition for which a campaign badge has been authorized. • Veterans who, while serving on active duty in the Armed Forces, participated in a military operation for which the Armed Forces Service Medal (AFSM) was awarded • Veterans separated from active duty within the past 3 years.
30% Disabled	Enables a hiring manager to appoint an eligible candidate to any position for which he or she is qualified, without competition. Unlike the VRA, there is no grade-level limitation.	• Disabled Veterans who were retired from active military service with a service-connected disability rating of 30 percent or more • Disabled Veterans rated by the Department of Veterans Affairs (VA) as having a compensable service-connected disability of 30 percent or more.
VEOA	• Gives preference eligible and certain eligible Veterans' access to jobs that otherwise only would have been available to status employees.	• Preference eligible • Service personnel separated after 3 or more years of continuous active service performed under honorable conditions.

Figure 4.2 | Civil Service Hiring Authorities for Veterans[5]

of the candidate during the application process to determine if you meet the KSAs for the position. Civil service hiring is also based on your capability to demonstrate your experience at the next lower level. So, if you are applying for a GS 12, your resume and questionnaire answers need to demonstrate your competencies and experience at the GS 11 level. Therefore, if you do not demonstrate your qualification for the position, your documentation will not be forwarded to the

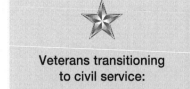

Veterans transitioning to civil service:

fedshirevets.gov/job-seekers/ special-hiring-authorities/#content

hiring official for review. Further information on answering federal self assessments can be found on monster.com.

Like other market places, there are significant advantages when it comes to mobility or being able to move to serve the needs of the government. When finding a position in a different locality you may receive pay for a move much like that in the military. Every position on USAJOBS.GOV will tell you if relocation is authorized. Sometimes, the department will offer relocation if it is hard to find someone with certain qualifications and/or interest in going to that particular location. For example, finding a job with relocation to the Washington D.C. area can be difficult. However, most rural locations without a significant local applicant pool will often provide relocation and/or financial incentive.

The best method for applying for civil service positions is through the comprehensive web site "USAJOBS.GOV". This web site not only posts jobs available by title description and location, it allows you to apply and track your application status. Helpful resume and application tips are given, enabling you to put your best foot forward.

GS Pay Tables:
https://www.opm.gov/
policy-data-oversight/
pay-leave/salaries-wages/salary-
tables/19Tables/html/DCB.aspx

Pay

Pay is a subject that is of great interest to all of us. Government Service (GS) pay scales operate on grade levels and geography. GS pay tables are standardized much like military pay tables, with the addition of locality pay adjustments. Therefore, you have to look at the correct scale for the location for which you are applying. As an example, Tampa has no special "locality pay area" table. In the case where there is no scale for the metropolitan area you are considering, look at the scale called "Rest of United States". Figure 4.3 below delineates the civil service pay scale for the San Jose, San Francisco area, including locality pay for step 1 through step 5. Remember, no locality pay is given in overseas areas. Instead, overseas employees receive cost of living allowances (COLA).

SALARY TABLE 20
INCORPORATING THE 1.4% GENERAL SCHEDULE INCRE
FOR THE LOCALITY PAY AREA OF WASHINGTON-BAL
TOTAL INCREASE:
EFFECTIVE JANUA
Annual Rates by Grade
Grade	**Step 1**	**Step 2**	**Step 3**	**Step 4**	**Step 5**	**Step**
1	$24,633	$25,458	$26,278	$27,091	$27,911	$28
2	27,696	28,356	29,273	30,049	30,386	31,
3	30,219	31,227	32,234	33,242	34,249	35
4	33,925	35,055	36,185	7,315	38,446	39,

Figure 4.3 | Pay & Leave: Salaries & Wages[6]

Benefits

A tremendous number of benefits are available to civil servants. Benefits are organized into five major categories: benefits and insurance, leave and work-life balance, pay and savings, retirement, and personnel records. There is some variety between agencies, and the country's economy plays a great role in the availability of some ben-

Civil servant benefits:

usa.gov/benefits-for-federal-employees

efits such as education. The major benefit categories are listed in Figure 4.4, but there are many benefits in each category. A complete detailed list is available at each agency web site and at www.usa.gov/FederalEmployees/ Benefits.shtml. Remember, not all benefits are available from each department or agency.

HIGH LEVEL BENEFITS FOR CIVIL SERVANTS

- Benefits and Insurance Programs
- Leave and Work-Life Balance
- Pay and Savings Plans
- Retirement
- Personnel Records

Figure 4.4 | Civil Service Benefits[7]

Department of Defense (DoD) Contracting Market Place

Many believe that the DoD contracting life blends the best of both attributes of GS and commercial market place while staying in a career supporting the military. The DoD contract environment is different from your military experience. You are still ultimately working for the defense of the nation, but you serve two masters. More importantly, the risk and rewards are both potentially greater than that of the civil service.

As a DoD contractor, you remain engaged with the defense of our nation. Many service members want to spend their post-military career doing something that feels familiar and comfortable. This is why many pursue DoD contracting after military service. Transitioning to a DoD contracting position gives you the comfort of a familiar language and a grasp on the needs of the mission and organization.[8]

Environment

For many, DoD contracting is a very appealing post military career. In addition to potentially better wages for your work efforts than civil service, you have the potential to stay within the same department or agency you already know and understand, while receiving significant flexibility not previously enjoyed. In most locations, you have the right to move on to another position or company should you become weary of your contract situation, bosses attitude, or government leadership. This knowledge and understanding provides relief for many in difficult or challenging situations.

Understanding the associated risks of DoD contracting is also very important. First, some find the government-contractor relationship challenging, especially after having been on the government side for a long period. If you choose to remain in the DoD environment, never lose site of the fact that the contractual relationship is adversarial by its very nature. There is goodness in this adversarial relationship. It is not only good for the taxpayer, but also provides constant checks and balances for both sides. The desire is to have a harmonious environment, with equilibrium between government overwatch and contract performance. If either side gains the upper hand, then a difficult and challenging work environment will exist.

"One of the most important but difficult tasks in contract administration is to develop a proper working relationship. Cooperation between the parties is essential if the work is to be successfully performed, and yet the parties are, in a very real sense, adversaries. The Government often attempts to obtain performance within the contract price, while the contractor attempts to maximize profits either by doing the minimum acceptable work or by attempting to obtain price increase."[9]

Why is this information important to you? Understanding the contract and government relationship is essential to your day-to-day life as a contractor. The question you face is how to deal with these types of relationship issues. Do you enjoy working through these types of challenges with contract leaders, program managers, and associated government counterparts? Some workers prefer running the contract (program management); others enjoy managing teams or projects (project management), while others like to perform work and provide service as a subject matter expert (SME) or task worker. It is important to find the right fit. Learning to understand the challenges that lie ahead and being prepared to identify them, process them, and create optional courses of action will help you be successful. Examples of challenges you will face as a DoD contractor are summarized below.

One of the first things you will have to reconcile as a new contractor is that most contracts have an estimated date for completion. This proves challenging for most former military folks as your term of service was relatively guaranteed. How to deal with uncertainty of follow on work with your contract can be challenging and stressful. This is potentially the contractor's greatest anxiety. Not only does the contractor have to perform well, satisfy the customer, accomplish the task or projects on time and to standard, but he or she must be keenly aware of the remaining contract duration and how well the contract at large is performing.

If you desire a steady income, you may find coping with this risk difficult. The contractors that feel most comfortable with this arrangement will typically grow a sizable rainy day fund (2-3 months' salary) to assist during contract transitional periods. This risk mitigation strategy will provide some peace of mind, especially in these challenging economic and ever changing political times. Always remember, that even in a down economy, the government remains the largest single employer in the country and there are plenty of contracting jobs available, especially if you are willing to relocate.

Another challenge to reconcile is that you will be working with either a military or a civil servant government lead. They will have the final say on decisions. Constrained by rules and regulations, the federal government is not famous for innovation or speed of bureaucratic consensus. These challenges may feel stifling or even frustrate some into choosing to move on to another occupation.

Opportunity

Like civil service, federal contractors receive similar benefits with regard to mobility, future work and security. Contracts extend well beyond Washington D.C., with departments, agencies and offices around the country, and around the world. That makes finding a job for those seeking a specific location, or desiring an opportunity to

Recruit Military:
Connecting organizations with veterans.
recruitmilitary.com

change localities, a great potential benefit. If you are mobile and good at what you do, the contract industry is going to have a job for you.[10] People move from job to job as contracts come and go. A DoD contracting career offers a significant chance for mobility and professional growth.[11]

Project diversity is an added benefit of being a DoD contractor. As you acquire a variety of experience, you will be increasingly sought after. You will have a chance to move in and out of various professional experiences. If you are already an expert in one area, working different projects means you will have the chance to develop new skills and explore potential new specialized areas.

Finally, like civil service, your security clearance is invaluable if you choose to stay in DoD contracting. If your clearance re-investigation date has passed and you have lost your clearance, but you have the experience needed, many contractors will offer to recapture your clearance as part of your hiring package. Additionally, many federal contractors will offer 'upgrades' of your clearance for required positions to meet certain contract requirements. You will not necessarily be reminded of your periodic investigation dates, so stay on top of your clearance. If a life event occurs such as financial issues, divorce, or arrest, make sure you inform your security officer quickly.

Job availability, good starting salaries and promotion potential are all positive aspects of contracting as long as you can go to where the jobs are. A defense contracting career is often the preference of many. If you have the skills wanted by the contractor at the right time, they will hire you on the spot with minimal paperwork and put you to work immediately. Further, you will have more control of your own destiny as your performance is the driving force in your career path. If you are performing, you will be promoted. If you are dissatisfied, then move to a more demanding job opportunity offering better pay.

Pay

As a contractor, you have a greater ability to negotiate a salary than your civil servant counter parts. As a company competes for new work with the government, a proposal is developed outlining various positions on the contract. The company will bid a specified price that takes into account a pay band for each position. Once awarded, the program manager has some flexibility within the pay band when hiring employees. This information may allow you to negotiate salary within the pay band for your desired position. Therefore, you will have to request a salary within a position's pay band, or you will probably not be hired.

As in the earlier quote from Sun Tzu, it is obvious the greatest road to success is to know yourself and know your environment.

Negotiating Salary?
See Appendix D or go to
GR8Transitions4U.com

It is often said the first party to mention a figure during salary negotiation will not fare as well in the negotiation. Therefore, when questioned about your salary requirements, it is best to ask about the pay band for your position and request a well thought out number that resides within that pay band. Appendix D of this book provides a method for determining a realistic salary request.

Benefits

First, know that human resource organizations will have specialists and experts that will explain and share current offerings in line with federal and state laws. Generally, there is minimal variation between contract companies when it comes to benefit packages. Regardless of which federal contractor you work for, you will find 100-150 hours offered as Paid Time Off (PTO) annually; or stated in military terms, leave. Of interest is that you accrue and take PTO by the hour and not by the day. This is helpful as you will need to take PTO occasionally for doctors' appointments, sick leave, or vacation. Unfortunately, most of the appointments that you go to during a military duty day will have to be charged as PTO. Another option, if available, is flex time. Many companies desire that you get 40 hours of work in one week or 80 hours over a two-week period. Often, you can flex hours within the pay period so that you could work 42 hours one week and 38 the next. This type of arrangement varies by company. Regardless, just remember that the time cards are archived for inspection by the Defense Contract Audit Agency (DCAA). Therefore, contract and personal integrity are on the line and the time card must accurately reflect hours worked.

With regards to health benefits, most companies offer comprehensive healthcare where you pay a share and the company pays a share. If you are a retiree, some companies adjust your salary if you utilize your retiree healthcare benefit. Just know, if you desire to use a company's healthcare you can, but there will more than likely be a deduction from your pay check for this benefit. Vision and dental are shared benefits as well. Just like your health insurance, if you are using TRICARE as an example, this benefit may not be of interest to you.

A flexible spending account is often available by larger companies in which you place some of your salary into an account for healthcare related expenditures.

The dollars you place in this program reduce your taxable income, but must all be used for healthcare by the end of each year. Most companies, big and small will offer a 401(k) plan for long-term retirement savings. These plans will generally be matching funds up to about 4-5%. The company will determine which investment group you will be buying into and you will generally have a choice of funds. Some companies allow all your dollars to be fully "vested" upon your initial investment. Others will allow you to have their matching funds after a vesting period has passed (i.e., 50% vested after 2 years, 100% after 3 years). These vesting periods vary considerably between companies. Just remember that the 401(k) is for long term retirement savings and significant penalties will normally be applied if you take out money prior to age 59½.[12] Additionally, some companies offer different types of stock options at discounted rates. This is an inexpensive way to invest in your company as you avoid brokerage fees in addition to any discount offered. Regardless, it is always recommended to place enough money in the 401(k) to get the matching funds, as you do not want to leave money on the table.

Larger companies have educational, training and certification assistance. Training authorization typically requires justification for the position you are in. Generally, companies will ask that you sign a document stating that you will not leave the company for some period of time (often 1 year) after taking the training dollars. This needs to be considered prior to taking training if you are thinking about changing companies, because some will hold back your last pay check to pay for your training if you have not completed the allotted time.

If you have not surmised, bigger DoD contract companies generally offer bigger and better benefits. The alternative is that smaller companies may have greater salary and might be more attractive to employees desiring fewer benefits. Therefore, if benefits are not that important and greater pay is a consideration, you may consider going to work for a smaller company. For example, if you have retiree benefits, you could negotiate more in salary. Finally, some small companies have greater flexibility for profit sharing with their employees. Regardless, weigh all of the benefits, salary, profit sharing and bonus capabilities to find the total compensation of the position. This exercise will assist you in weighing your options when comparing multiple job offers.

Commercial Market Place

Transitioning into the commercial market place from the military requires considerable great risk tolerance and a high level of confidence in your ability to perform in a competitive environment. As mentioned at the beginning of this chapter, workers in commercial firms are three times more likely to be fired as compared to federal employees. Working in the commercial market is not for the faint of heart, and the risks must be managed. However, most working in the commercial market quickly state that the rewards for this risk outweigh the job security of civil service.

Environment

Because workers strive for personal growth and reward, the commercial environment is often very competitive. In the commercial environment, employees generally try to remain competitive through innovation and providing business value to the organization. This determination and drive often require numerous man hours above and beyond a traditional 40 hour work week. Understandably, most workers join the commercial market place to earn significant amounts of money, to be trained or gain experience, positioning themselves to earn significant money later.

It is always the desire in commercial market to achieve profitability and make money. Maximizing profit will drive all business decisions. If there are two choices, the best business case will be selected. Companies and managers will consistently pursue the highest potential profit at the best value every time they make a business decision. What this means to you as a potential worker in the commercial environment is that you must understand this concept and remain viable to the company, otherwise your services will not be needed for long. The profit concept is foreign to most public sector workers, including service members. Be advised, this concept sometimes becomes a bias against hiring veterans for some commercial hiring managers.

In high performing companies, there is tremendous focus on the bottom line. Managers desire to achieve this focus which leads to well understood, top to bottom goals and objectives. Two most important objectives driving decision making in the commercial market place are solution and price. Focusing on solution and price typically drives satisfaction and value in the commercial market. Managers must focus on providing and creating added value through the products and services offered by their company. The best solution is sought, as it increases return on investment and profit. Therefore, you need to be synchronized with management as you are held accountable for your work, and you are rewarded for success and potentially fired for failure.[13]

Therefore, understand what drives value in your work environment. Knowing this will help you align your day-to-day work effort as you deal with the customer as well as connect better when looking for a job. Nothing is more nerve racking than going to an interview or giving a presentation and not understanding how your employer perceives or derives value. Further, you are far better off talking to your leadership about their view regarding the best solution and profit, rather than deriving unfinanced requirements and perceived cost savings which do not aid the organization's bottom line.

Opportunity

The commercial sector is set apart from the public sector with regard to rapid personal growth potential for achievers, with financial reward and the promise of a creative and innovative environment. Rapid change is pervasive with the ever-changing business environment, and you will be rewarded if you embrace and become part of the change. One of the great attributes associated with the commercial market place is that your high performance will enable you to progress quickly without regard to a pay scale or longevity. As you work on your professional goals and career path, utilize opportunities to gain additional and diverse experience. Seek out ways to gain internal qualifications through training that aligns with your career goals. Keep in mind where you want to be and take on challenges to posture yourself for future success.

Financial reward is based largely on your ability to remain viable and valuable to the organizations. If you are adding to the bottom line you will be rewarded financially. The company rewards your positive impact and participation. Companies know that if you move on, they may lose profit and key knowledge to the competition.

Innovation and creativity are also well rewarded in the private sector, as long as the innovation adds to the company's competitiveness, market position, or bottom line.

Remember, to remain competitive, companies will seek innovative workers and will make change based on the business environment. If you like an exciting and dynamic environment, the commercial sector is for you.

Pay

Conventional wisdom has it that you'll always make more money in the commercial market place, with lower pay being the trade-off for job security in the federal government.

That's generally true. The Federal Salary Council, a group of union officials and pay policy experts, says federal workers overall earn about 35 percent less than their commercial-sector peers.[14]

Another aspect to remember is that your project management experience from the military, if understood by your civilian hiring manager, will assist in landing a good paying job. On average, you will enjoy 20% more pay, if you have the PMP credential as discussed in Chapter Three. Further, you will be able to demand higher pay in the commercial market place with every year of experience you have acquired.[15]

Benefits

In general, benefits are similar or better than DoD contracting. The one exception is small business as, you may have fewer benefits. That being said, even small businesses must offer the following benefits as they are considered mandatory by the federal government.[16]

- Time off to vote, serve on a jury and perform military service.
- Comply with all workers' compensation requirements.
- Withhold FICA taxes from employees' paychecks and pay your own portion of FICA taxes, providing employees with retirement and disability benefits.
- Pay state and federal unemployment taxes, thus providing benefits for unemployed workers.
- Contribute to state short-term disability programs in states where such programs exist.
- Comply with the Federal Family and Medical Leave (FMLA).

Surprisingly, the following benefits are not required to be given to employees and you may see a variation of these benefits at every company.

- Retirement plans
- Health plans
- Dental or vision plans
- Life insurance plans
- Paid vacations, holidays or sick leave

Having said all of this, most large companies offer tremendous benefits and some unexpected surprises upon arrival. Price Waterhouse Coopers (PWC)[17] advertises the following perks on their web site:

- **Sabbatical:** Employees can take four-week sabbaticals with 20 percent to 50 percent of pay.
- **Tuition Reimbursement and Scholarships:** At PWC, employees can get up to $5,250 in financial assistance to further their education.
- **401(k):** PWC contributes 5 percent of an employees' annual pay to their 401(k) retirement savings plans even if they don't make their own contribution.
- **Volunteer Hours:** Every employee receives 10 hours per year of paid time off to volunteer for charities of their choice.
- **Rewards and Recognitions:** Employees can earn contribution awards when managers or partners recognize them for excellence, outstanding effort and team work.

Non-Profit Organizations - FFRDC/UARC

A Nonprofit Organization (NPO) functions with a purpose or function, other than making a profit. NPOs are typically dedicated to furthering a social cause or advocating ideals.

FFRDC are unique nonprofit entities sponsored and funded by the U.S. government. The Federal Acquisition Regulation (FAR) requires they operate in the public interest free from organizational conflicts of interest and can therefore assist in ways that industry contractors cannot. FFRDCs assist with governmental scientific research and analysis, systems development, and systems acquisition. FFRDCs operate in the industries of defense, homeland security, energy, aviation, space, health and human services, and tax administration. FFRDCs are grouped into three categories focusing on different types of activities:

- System engineering and integration centers
- Study and analysis centers
- Research and development centers (includes national laboratories)

FFRDCs were established to provide the DoD with unique analytical, engineering, and research capabilities in many areas where the government cannot attract and retain personnel in sufficient depth and numbers. Currently, there are over 40 recognized FFRDCs sponsored by the U.S. government. University Affiliated Research Centers (UARC) are strategic DoD research centers associated with one or more universities.

More Information:
nonprofitready.org

If you decide to go this route, an NPO wants to know that you are truly interested in their cause and what they are doing – just as much as the skills that you have. You may show your loyalty to the cause and your interest by starting out with the organization as a volunteer.

Entrepreneurship

As mentioned earlier in the chapter, the subject of entrepreneurship is only lightly discussed. There are many resources available for this sector as there are many variations of start-up businesses. For example, you might want to start a consulting firm or a project management firm

For More Info:
va.gov/osdbu/entrepreneur/

as a disabled veteran or minority owned business. Additionally, each city/county/state offers a variety of classes and seminars on how to successfully start these types of companies. If you should try entrepreneurship as a consultant or business, keep in mind the following concepts:

- You must be willing to take on risk to achieve success.
- There is no cook book and you cannot be a quitter.
- You need to have deep pockets or backing.
- Take time to understand the business, taxation, government laws, and contracting associated with the business you are going pursuing.
- The measure of success for entrepreneurship is survivability 5 to 10 years out.
- Entrepreneurship is tough on the family and quality of life, unless there are other sources of income.
- You must be an optimist and pride yourself on doing things differently.

Market Place Comparison

Understanding how the commercial market place differs from the government is absolutely essential for your success in transitioning from the military. Knowing the value proposition is essential. Public organizations will perceive value through mission accomplishment, with the least amount of hassle or disturbance. Private organizations will find value through seeking out the least cost and greatest capability, thereby enhancing the bottom line.

When looking at this question from the employee perspective, a term coined in England when comparing the public and private market place is "Sector Envy". Universally, it appears that the "Grass is always greener" when looking at the opposing market place. With wildly varying risks, rewards, salaries, benefits and job security, "Sector Envy" is a very appropriate term among American workers as well. Let's compare the public and private market place as they relate to your personal desires.

With regard to "Sector Envy" it is interesting to note that there is an increase in the migration of workers moving back and forth between government agencies, DoD contractors and the commercial market place. Employees with contracting backgrounds make easy transitions into federal and civil servant jobs due to their skills, knowledge and abilities (SKAs). Generally, as a former service member becomes more familiar with the commercial sector and obtains certification, they become more marketable. Know that many have come before you and not only changed jobs, but also market places on multiple occasions.

So what do you need to know? You should be aware that there are many factors that separate public and private sectors. Fundamental environmental factors include: value proposition, business case, turnover challenges, and measures of success. Obvious personal factors are financial rewards, job security, benefits, and your ability to easily transition from the service. Some of the not so obvious factors are work-life balance, changing work environment, workload and career ladder. A few comparative environmental factors are given below:

Value proposition - Private sector managers worry about creating added value, while public-sector managers are often stifled by outdated, restrictive laws, regulations and policies that prevent rapid change or action.

Business case - In private industry there are clear well understood top to bottom goals and objectives. In the public sector goals are often divergent or disparate and can lead to confusion.

Turnover challenges - In government, leaders are often rotated in and out to ensure proper grooming and development of leadership. This thrash of leadership creates potential organizational change based on personality rather than achieving unity of movement towards goals and objectives. The corollary in the business world is a business merger or hostile takeover.

Key Performance Indicators (KPI) – In the absence of clearly understood business goals, government often invents measures of success that might be more aligned to short-term contractual and personal goals versus long-term business goals.

Stone walling – In the government setting, if a leader is not well received, senior civil servants will slow roll and wait out leadership change. This is especially true for political appointees or temporary military leadership. In the private sector there is no business case for this type of activity, as most companies would find this unacceptable.

These fundamental factors have huge environmental implications on workplace satisfaction. Figure 4.5 below compares positive responses from federal government employees against commercial-sector workers. These questions reflect the impact of some environmental factors previously discussed. The results show the public sector holds a slight edge over the commercial market place when employees are asked if they like the kind of work they do.[18] However, when it comes to recognition, training and supervisors, the commercial market place employees are a big winner.

QUESTION	GOVERNMENT-WIDE	COMMERCIAL MARKET PLACE	GAP
I like the kind of work I do.	81.2	75.0	6.2
My work gives me a feeling of personal accomplishment.	69.7	70.0	-0.3
I have enough information to do my job well.	69.3	71.0	-1.7
The people I work with cooperate to get the job done.	72.3	78.0	-5.7
I am given a real opportunity to improve my skills in my organization.	59.6	66.0	-6.4
Overall, how good a job do you feel is being done by your immediate supervisor/ team leader?	65.8	73.0	-7.2
How satisfied are you with your opportunity to get a better job in your organization?	31.5	44.0	-12.5
How satisfied are you with the training you receive for your present job?	46.6	61.0	-14.4
How satisfied are you with the information you receive from management on what's going on in your organization?	44.8	60.0	-15.2
How satisfied are you with the recognition you receive for doing a good job?	42.6	64.0	- 21.4

Figure 4.5 | Comparison - Federal to Commercial Work Satisfaction

Personal Market Place Satisfaction Scale

Having read the environmental factors, a side by side Market Place Satisfaction Scale is presented for your understanding of the remaining factor differences. When looking at the market places for future opportunities, it is beneficial to optimize where you search. Most of us do not have the latitude of time on our side to look for and, more importantly get a job. You can spend months searching through the job listings. Unfortunately, about 20% of people leave their jobs every year, according to the Bureau of Labor Statistics.

If it is important for you not to be part of the statistic and continually rotate jobs, there are a few items to consider. A key consideration to staying in a particular job is your personal satisfaction. Sometimes we forget the "personal satisfaction" factor, as this will increase the chances of remaining in the same position. Make an honest evaluation and list the factors necessary for your workdays to be as enjoyable and rewarding as possible.

Nine satisfaction elements are utilized in the personal satisfaction scale. The definition of each element used in this tool is defined in Figure 4.6.

FACTOR	DEFINITION
Creative Environment	Opportunity/need to be creative in the job.
Financial Reward	Probability of salary increase and bonus based on success.
Change	Frequency of change expected on the job to maintain position.
Workload	Level of work expected to perform on the job to sustain position.
Career Ladder	Clearly defined job growth expectations and requirements.
Education Reimbursement	Financial reimbursement for additional education and certifications.
Work/Life Balance	Based upon rules and work week expectations, presents a level of work/life balance important to keep personnel satisfied.
Job Risk	Volatility and chance of losing your job due to issues outside of your control.
Benefits	Level of standardized benefits to include medical/dental, savings, retirement, vacation time, education, etc.
Ease of Transition	Determination of transitional ease for former service members.

Figure 4.6 | Factor Definitions

To assist in your organization of these personal satisfaction elements, the following market place satisfaction scale is presented. Columns represent the four market places covered in this chapter: Civil Service, DoD Contractor, Commercial, and Entrepreneur. Rows represent typical elements as they relate to the market place. The scale is presented below in Figure 4.7. Probabilities are plotted for each factor in each marketplace based upon whether the element has a high-medium-low likelihood of influence in the marketplace. Data for the grid is based upon many years of discussion and experience among veterans. There will always be exceptions, but for your purposes, the table should prove helpful to those in transition from the military, offering a foundation that can be customized based upon your own experiences.

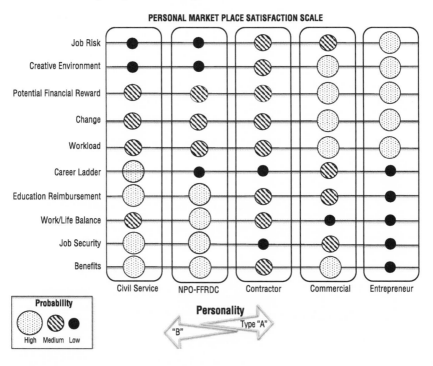

Figure 4.7 | Personal Market Place Satisfaction

At a glance, two items that might be of importance to you are security and work/life balance. If these two are important to you, you may gravitate towards the civil service work. If you enjoy risk and desire a highly competitive and potentially creative environment, you may align yourself with commercial industry, or perhaps, even entrepreneurship.

When considering all the elements of the table, you will notice that the civil service marketplace offers more stability and you can have relative confidence that you will be able to remain in the position, with a standard offering of benefits, salary and a pro-active work/life balance. If you desire to climb the corporate ladder and create an opportunity of accelerated promotions and desire to try to capture a better than average salary due to your creative mindset, you will be better served in either the Commercial of Entrepreneurial markets.

Finally, the scale roughly correlates with personality types. You may have previously identified with either 'Type A' or 'Type B' behaviors. 'Type A' personalities are typically ambitious, rigidly organized, high achieving, "workaholics", multi-taskers, highly motivated, insist on deadlines, and hate both delays and ambivalence.

Contrastingly, 'Type B' personalities live at a lower stress level and typically work steadily, enjoying achievement but do not become stressed if immediate gratification is not present. They may be creative and enjoy exploring ideas and concepts and are often reflective.

Use Figure 4.7 to assist you in developing thoughts on which market place may provide the best landing space for you after the service based on your personality and style. Take a few moments and ponder the difference to ensure you are pursuing the best match for your lifestyle.

Assessment #5 *(Market Place)*

Figure 4.8 is the fifth and final assessment in the book, exploring personal factors that influence which market place to offer the most alignment to your interests. You may answer the assessment questions here. When you are ready to analyze them, refer to Chapter Five. You can also utilize the companion guide to this book, available for download and print out at Gr8Transitions4U.com. Read each question and choose the correct answer for your current situation.

5: MARKET PLACE	Strongly Disagree	Disagree	Neither Agree OR Disagree	Agree	Strongly Agree
I am aware of my personal stress tolerance, as it relates to each market place.					
I understand the relationship between job, risks and rewards with regard to the market place.					
I have compared and contrasted the associated benefits of each market place.					
I have studied the workplace nuances associated with each market place.					
I have analyzed how well I would transition into each market place.					
I have looked at the pros and cons of job stability, change and longevity within each market place.					
I have researched career progression within each market place.					
I have discussed market place decisions with my significant other.					
I have analyzed each market place with regard to my short and long term personal goals and objectives.					
I have compared the market places against my personal desires for work life balance.					

Figure 4.8 | Market Place Assessment

Summary

Once comfortable with the basics, knowledge of the market place will help you gain a competitive advantage and keep you from proceeding down the wrong path for your next career. A few departing thoughts are presented as you progress in your job search and transition:

1. If you have a target market place in mind, make sure your resume is tailored to the market you desire and that your network and connections will be able to assist.

2. Inquire and ask questions at the end of an interview such as: how the company views different positions, how risk adverse the company is, how mature their documentation processes are, what tools are used, what career path options are open to someone starting in your position, and what criteria is used to measure and advance.

3. Once at the job, think out-of-the-box. Do not just go into the job and expect a list of daily activities to perform. In the military, you had to adapt. Now is the time to utilize that trait.

4. Gain confidence in the new position by understanding both the official and unofficial political fabric of your environment.

5. Understand your peers and your boss(es). As you master your expected job skills, continue to branch out as far as possible to other divisions, groups, and teams. This knowledge will increase your overall understanding and appreciation of the organization, as a holistic view will assist you in evaluating the position you are in and how it connects with your expectations and goals.

The choice to prepare yourself and perform good market place selection, is yours to make. You are encouraged to continue to grow your understanding of these different sectors. In the following story, discover how a veteran, after working in commercial market, as a DoD contractor, and a civil servant, finally found a home that best met his personality type. When asked about which side of the fence he would rather be on, former Army Sergeant Joel Taylor stated "It all depends upon the position."

You will find the best work environment as well!

Joel Taylor
Perseverance and Flexibility

*Joel Taylor understands and is proud of his humble begin-
nings as the son of an enlisted soldier. He believes military
kids are resilient, well versed and persevere under dire circumstances. Joel remembers lean times and his father's
difficult adjustment to civilian life after retirement. He clearly
recalls his father's euphoria when he finally landed a civil
service position at the local base.*

*After enlisting in the Army as an aviation operations spe-
cialist, Joel's first assignment was overseas. Understanding
the importance of education and training, Joel volunteered
for every school available. In addition, he quickly learned
going to schools kept him out of "the field" and allowed him
to maximize time with his new bride. After making Sergeant, Joel was accepted for flight school, but was going
to have to take a reenlistment and hardship assignment to
Korea without his new wife. Not wanting the separation,
Joel made a decision to get out of the service, which he
would question for many years.*

*Joel followed his wife in her dreams of becoming an Air
Force officer. After moving to Phoenix with his wife and
meeting a new circle of her professional friends, Joel set
his sights on furthering his education. Joel began utilizing
the VA Work Study Program, working at the local Family
Support Center on base, while studying computer science.
Eighteen months later he had completed the MCSE (Microsoft Certified Systems Engineer) and the CCNA (Cisco
Certified Network Associate) programs.*

*During a brief assignment in Europe with his wife, Joel
continued his education at night, while working during the
day as a "support assistant" for the Department of Defense*

Dependents Schools (DoDDS). It is here that Joel got his first taste of managing projects while working facilities maintenance projects.

Returning to the states, Joel had finished a Bachelor's degree and found a contract position as a network administrator and IT trainer, utilizing his information technology certifications at MacDill Air Force Base.

At this point, Joel was at an impasse. Was he to gain more IT certification training or to get the master's degree he had always desired? Joel decided to use the G.I. Bill to get his M.B.A., deciding he would rather lead the team than engineer the solutions. He also chose to remain current with his certifications, but was called out at an interview for not yet having a "PMP".

Believing that the PMP was the next major career move to gain confidence in his ability to maintain the quality life style he and his family desired, Joel pursued the PMP. Making "one of the best decisions ever", Joel paid for the training and testing out of his own pocket as the company he was working for refused. Suddenly with a MBA, lots of computer certifications, work experience and the PMP, Joel was getting weekly job calls. He confidently states that his "employment offers doubled" after obtaining the PMP.

Subsequently, Joel worked as a contractor for many years. He worked and led many types of projects, programs and proposal efforts. He found that the contract life, with the concerns of layoffs and inability to be in charge of the situation frustrating. He found himself asking if he "really wants to be one of the corporate guys?" Trusting himself, Joel applied for a few civil service jobs and three months later took a pay cut as a government program manager for United States Special Operations Command (USSOCOM).

Today, Joel has no regrets. He has worked hard and continues his education every way possible, pursuing required Defense Acquisition University (DAU) courses. Joel believes civil service benefits, eliminating multiple bosses, and being empowered to make decisions that matter, are all well worth the cut in pay. Now he "leads the team" and believes he has found his niche. Interestingly, even after great success, Joel still states that he does not know what he will do next; but he knows he is not done.

5

The Right Fit

NOW IT IS YOUR TURN.

While reading this book you have gained focus of your strengths, simultaneously learning about the job market and the project management profession. You have the logic behind positioning yourself for the job market and your next career. You have gained the confidence to attack the competition. Now you will organize these elements together to shift your mental posture from the defensive to the offensive.

Combining the knowledge gained from this book with the personal information you collected through the assessments will facilitate the creation of a high impact personal strategic roadmap. This exciting instrument provides directed self-awareness while gaining an under-

> *"One defends when his strength is inadequate, he attacks when it is abundant"*
>
> **Sun Tzu 孫子**
> *The Art of War*

standing of your strengths and the confidence required to take on the next challenge.

Several tools are introduced in this chapter. The first tool is for charting of your assessment scores collected in earlier chapters. This tool identifies those personal areas that can be exploited (strengths) and those areas for possible improvement. The second tool is the Personal Strategic Roadmap. Assessment scores that reflect areas for possible improvement will be transferred onto your personal strategic roadmap. This roadmap will be used continuously as you track, monitor, and achieve your personal goals.

To gain the best results, work through the process with honest introspection and reflection. Completing these steps enable you to identify preference for market place, career and level of readiness for transitioning into project management. There are three steps involved:

1. Gaining an understanding and control of personal information and capabilities that you have, thereby reducing risks of the unknown.

2. Analyzing outcomes of each assessment to identify what you already possess in your "kit bag" for successful resume writing, interviewing, and transition.

3. Setting goals based on those areas you choose for improvement. These improvements are to be charted, monitored, and tracked on the Personal Strategic Roadmap until they are achieved.

Step One - Gaining Control of Your Personal Information (The UNK-UNK Chart)

In certain areas of the military and civilian world, the UNK-UNK chart is used to depict information available about organizations. The title of the UNK-UNK chart is derived from using "UNK" as an abbreviation to "Unknown". The chart is useful not only to military planning and operation groups, but to commercial organizations performing risk analysis. When you transform an organizational construct to a personal perspective, the UNK-UNK chart is useful in identifying and understanding what you know and don't know about yourself.

The UNK-UNK chart is broken into four quadrants (Figure 5.1). Quadrants are defined with regard to the terms "Known" and "Unknown". These terms refer to a general understanding of information an organization has awareness of ("knowns") and information not known ("unknowns"). When you array these two terms on both sides of the chart and step through the following analysis, an approach to reducing your "unknowns" begins to unfold. Organizations categorize information as follows: What information they know (KK); what they know that they don't know (KU); what they do not know that they know

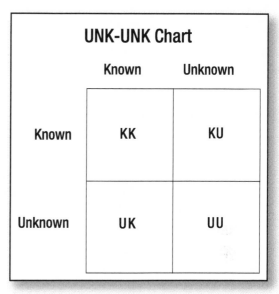

Figure 5.1 | UNK-UNK Chart

(UK); and what information they do not know exists and are completely unaware of (UU).

The upper left quadrant (KK-information you know you know) is a very valuable commodity. In this quadrant, the organization is "self-aware" and this knowledge can be exploited. By way of a military example, if you know you know the location of the enemy, you plan and move to contact to destroy the enemy at this location. Similarly, in business, a corporation would want to try to exploit its capabilities in the marketplace if they knew they had a competitive advantage. From a personal perspective, your skills, characteristics, abilities, and sense for the type of marketplace you want to pursue are very valuable. Acknowledge and exploit this information on your resume and during your interviews to achieve the best career alignment.

The upper right quadrant (KU, or, know what you do not know) denotes an organization, which understands they do not have certain information elements needed for success. Capturing these information elements provides tremendous value for study, assessment and improvement within the organization. For example, if a company does not have market information they consider valuable, they work to resolve the information shortfall in an effort to gain a competitive advantage. From a personal perspective, knowing that you do not have a capability is of vital importance. During an interview, not knowing the hiring manager's expectations and how the organization perceives value can bring the interview process to a halt. Take some time to know the customer to try and reduce the risk associated with this quadrant. KU elements become goals for your Personal Strategic Roadmap. Achieving these associated goals turn KUs into KKs, increasing your competitive edge.

The bottom left quadrants (UK, or, you don't know what you know), is very harmful in combat. To avoid this outcome, military organizations employ a term or slogan "Who else needs to know?" When critical information is not shared, it can cause mission failure. A company may know they have a capability, but fail to see its value or how to exploit the capability, and their competitor gets to market faster. Applying this quadrant to your personal transition, you want to ensure you have uncovered your capabilities, even the ones that you do not expect to be of significant marketability. During interviews, take time to exploit and share your accomplishments, certifications, and experiences as they relate to the company.

Finally, the bottom right quadrant (UU, or information you don't know that you don't know) is all about reaction. "Ignorance is bliss" is a common cliché associated with this quadrant. In this quadrant, action occurs and change happens rapidly if you do not have the information necessary for counter-action. It is the riskiest of quadrants as there are unexpected outcomes, because you could not anticipate events. In the corporate world, while you

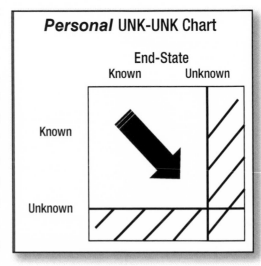

Figure 5.2 | Competitive Gain

continue the status quo, your competitor may develop something viable and exploit the market opportunity before you ever realize what happened!

Why go through the exercise of analyzing the UNK-UNK chart? Your objective is to reduce the size of any unknowns and associated risks. As shown in Figure 5.2, reducing the level of "unexpected unknowns" and turning them into "knowns" is the best method to increase your personal edge and confidence. There will always be "unknown" shortcomings, but it is essential to reduce the 'unknown' quadrant as much as possible by expanding other quadrants, making your 'known' area as large as possible. For this to happen, reflect upon your undiscovered skills and characteristics.

With the knowledge of the UNK-UNK chart, let us use the remaining tools of this book to help you determine what areas you need to exploit and what you need to improve upon.

Step Two - Understanding Assessment Results

Analyzing assessment outcomes assists in determining what you already have in your "kit bag" for transitional success. In each prior chapter, assessments were provided in five key transitional areas, summarized in Figure 5.3. As mentioned in the introduction, your assessment results should have been documented in the gem formats, available through the free downloadable companion guide found at GR8Transitions4U.com.

Assessment Type	Chapter	Topic Areas
Personal Characteristics	2	Leadership, motivation, creativity, managing others, personal growth, organizational skills, repeatability, working with others, visionary
Environmental	2	Family, re-locations, financial obligations, retirement objectives, schools, faith, etc.
Timing	2	Service goals met, training/certification goals, time remaining, commitment, financial preparedness
Skills	3	Military skills, educations, certifications, credentials, jobs
Market Place	4	Civil Service, contractor (DoD), commercial market place, analysis based on income, stress competition predictability, longevity, mental growth, benefits

Figure 5.3 | Assessment Topics

Star Charting

To assess your strengths and improvement areas, a chart in the form of a star will be created utilizing the companion guide. Begin building the star by charting each assessment score on a 'gem' (Figure 5.4) on the y-axis. The y-axis represents your readiness to transition; or how 'ready' you are to transition from the military. For each assessment, use the question number and plot answer results on each gem axis. It is highly recommended that you use the free companion guide for star charting. However, the five gems and the star can be manually recreated.

When plotting the results of your assessments, you will likely find more than one answer on an axis point. Simply cluster the plotted points. Analysis of each assessment gem offers a journey to unfolding your personal roadmap. In turn, the roadmap will guide you to the best-suited career path in the best-suited market place.

Companion Guide at:
GR8Transitions4U.com

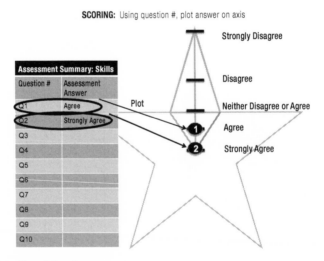

Figure 5.4 | Star Chart Mapping

Once each gem is completed, combine all gems with the associated assessment results to build the Star Chart provided in the companion guide to view your aggregate results (Figure 5.5).   When combined, these plotted assessment results form the shape of a star, resulting in a personal index.   Your personal index summarizes key indicators from your personal, environmental, timing, marketplace and skills assessments; clearly stating your readiness, marketplace, and ease of transition from the military. With this knowledge you will understand the best options to pursue, given your strategy goals and objectives.

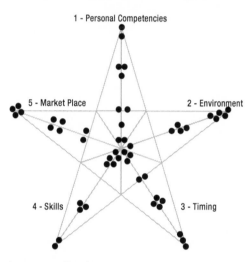

Figure 5.5 | Star Chart Assessment Results

Within the star is the shape of a pentagon (Figure 5.6). Assessment answers plotted within the pentagon represent your strengths. These strengths must be captured and are items to be exploited in your job search and interviews. Assessment answers plotted outside of the pentagon suggest that these are potential areas important to improve, and to be transferred to your Personal Strategic Roadmap discussed in Step Three. Once the analysis of your assessment answers has been completed, you are ready to move on to creating your personal strategic roadmap.

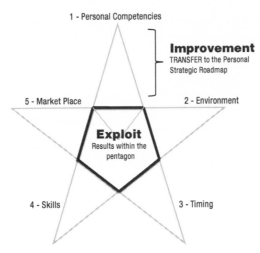

Figure 5.6 | Star Chart Areas for Improvement and Exploitation

Step Three - Setting Your Goals

Next, use the Personal Strategic Roadmap to capture your noted areas of improvement from the assessments and increase your probability of transition success. The outcome of this step will be the Personal Strategic Roadmap shown in Appendix E. A full size, editable Personal Strategic Roadmap is also available in the free online companion guide. There are four main sections to the roadmap as shown in Figure 5.7.

Personal Strategic Roadmap Sections	
1.	Improvements
2.	Vision
3.	Goals and Success
4.	Commit and Attest

Figure 5.7 | Strategic Roadmap Sections

Use the Personal Strategic Roadmap to list your goals and establish how you will achieve these goals, along with setting the target timeframes for each goal. It is on your roadmap that you will track and monitor these goals until achieved. You will need to monitor your goals on a recurring basis and track your progress. As goals are met, reward yourself, remove each of them from the roadmap and transfer each of these goals to your resume or exploit during your next interview.

Follow the next repeatable actions to complete each critical section of the roadmap and gain the full benefit.

a. Section 1 - Capture Improvements:

As mentioned in Step 2, identify all assessment answers outside of the pentagon. Transfer these improvements to the top portion of the roadmap in the improvements section. It is important to capture all improvements from all assessments. For example, plotted results from the Skills Assessment Gem determine a need to achieve a commercial project management certification, like the PMP®. In the improvements section of the Personal Strategic Road Map, list those items in Part 4, skills as shown in Figure 5.8 below:

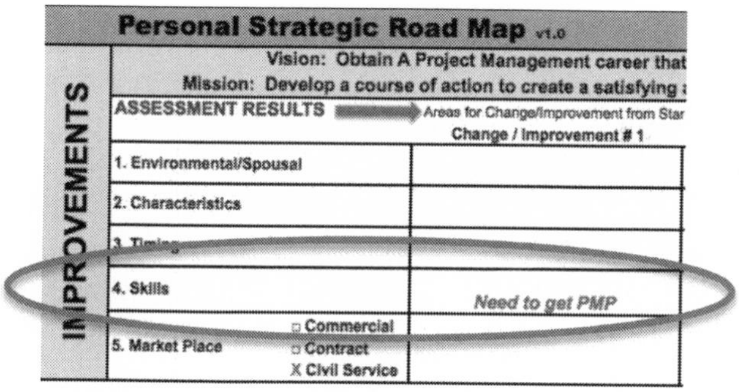

Figure 5.8 | Strategic Map Improvements

b. Section 2 - State your personal Vision:

Based upon your reading and the improvements captured from Section 1, reflect upon how you desire to work on these improvements. Some of the improvements might be independent of others, such as your interest to take a class to achieve a certification. Some improvements might be best combined with others. For example, you may desire to focus your job search in the Civil Service market place and geographically target your job search to the northeast

131

region of the United States where you can be close to a major airport. To adequately capture the influences in achieving your personal vision, write what you want to achieve with the qualifiers that are important to you in the vision section. Include some or all of the following: Job place/location (CONUS/OCONUS, state, city), timeframe, marketplace focus, salary range, possible positions, risk level you are willing to take, industries, and any other considerations. An example is given in Figure 5.9 as follows:

VISION	VISION: Based upon your reading and the 5 assessment areas above, restate your job objectives to include some or all of the following: Job place/location (CONUS/OCONUS, state/city, timeframe, marketplace focus, salary range, possible positions, risk level you are willing to take, industries, and any other considerations
	YOUR VISION: Make myself marketable for a project management career in the Civil Service market place in the northeast region of the U.S. with a major airport nearby. By mid-2015, I want to have my resume reflect my credentials and all my project experience.

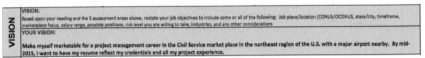

Figure 5.9 | Strategic Map Vision

c. Section 3 - Create Goals and identify Success:

Now you will create goals from your areas of improvement. If there are more than four improvements, it is recommended that you focus on three or four most important to you. Further, take into consideration the level of effort and time associated with the success of achieving the goal. Some improvement/goals might be independent of one another, such as your interest to take a class to achieve a certification. Some improvement/goals might be best grouped with one or more improvements to clarify and better define success. Transform your improvements into goals that can be achieved with an identified timeframe and measured. For example, transform the improvement 'get a project management certification' to the goal of 'Get PMI PMP® certification'. Post the steps you need to take to achieve the goal, as well as a specific timeframe that you want to achieve the goal as shown in Figure 5.10 below.

GOALS & ACHIEVEMENT

GOALS:
Pick most important improvement areas from above you want to focus on, depending on level of complexity, learning, or duration (i.e., school).
* List: goals, align which Assessment it ties, year/quarter/month expected to achieve, and present your achievement path (how you will get to your goal and possible steps if necessary

PRIORITY	GOAL Statement	ASSESSMENT TIE	PATH TO ACHIEVING GOAL	YEAR/QTR/MO TO ACHIEVE (personally set)				ACHIEVED ?
GOAL # 1	*Get PMI PMP® Certification*	__ Environment __ Characteristics __ Timing X Skills __ Market Place	** I will research military classes for PMP, study, apply for certification, take exam and pass!*	Q1 2015 - class	Q2 2015 - App	Q3 2015 exam	certificate	YES / NO Reschedule or no longer need? Date ______
GOAL # 2		__ Environment __ Characteristics __ Timing __ Skills __ Market Place						YES / NO Reschedule or no longer need? Date ______
GOAL # 3		__ Environment __ Characteristics __ Timing __ Skills __ Market Place						YES / NO Reschedule or no longer need? Date ______
GOAL # 4		__ Environment __ Characteristics __ Timing __ Skills __ Market Place						YES / NO Reschedule or no longer need? Date ______

Figure 5.10 | Strategic Map Goals and Achievement

Set a reminder through your calendar to review your progress on each goal listed. Depending on the urgency of the goal, review your roadmap weekly. Do this religiously and do not falter. Look at your roadmap and ask yourself – "What progress or steps have I taken to move towards achieving this goal?" Once progress is achieved, make notes in the path to achieving goal. If there are outside circumstances that have caused a slip to the right of your scheduled achievement – annotate and move on. Ask yourself was it a slip based upon not working to achieve the goal, or an outside circumstance that was out of your control? Assess the situation and adjust your goal schedule accordingly in the 'year/quarter/month' to achieve area. If you achieve the goal – mark 'yes' and celebrate! You are that much closer to an easier and successful transition.

d. Section 4 - Commit and Attest:

Once you identify what you want to do, annotate it, then sign and date the roadmap as shown in Figure 5.11 below. If you have a family member or a mentor you want to watch and monitor with you, get them to co-sign. Why? You need to remind yourself and your family that you are committed to achieving these goals and that you want to remain accountable. Make a copy of this form and hang it on your refrigerator, or keep it in your wallet. Remind yourself and your family that everyone is working together on achieving these goals. Set a repeatable time for a thorough review of your personal strategic roadmap, preferably with the cosigner and revisit the courses of actions if necessary.

While this is a roadmap that captures the steps you need to transition from the military, the goals themselves are not cast in stone. If for some reason a goal becomes overcome by events, do not see this as a failure. Carefully assess the situation and the circumstances surrounding the reason why the goal is not achievable and take it off the list. Revisit Sections A through D and transform other improvement areas as they develop into goals. Through achieving these goals, you will increase your 'knowns', thereby increasing your opportunity for job transition and success.

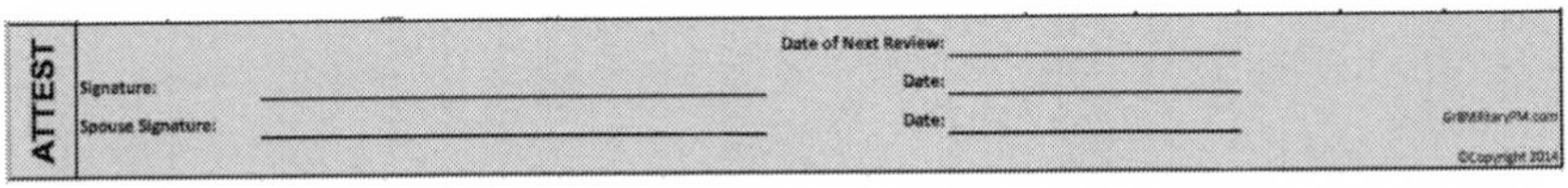

Figure 5.11 | Strategic Map Sign and Attest

Summary

In chapter five you gained an understanding of your strengths and weaknesses as identified in the assessments provided earlier in the book. These weaknesses are marked for improvement and are translated into goals and annotated in the Personal Strategic Roadmap. Your strengths become areas to highlight on a resume and in an interview.

The bottom line is to increase your "knowns" and reduce the risk of the "unknowns" through preparation, planning and analysis. The more assessment results within the pentagon, the higher probability that you are ready to transition with minimum issues and stress. Use your strategic roadmap to achieve areas of improvement and increase your personal "knowns". This actionable exercise will increase the probability of success as you look and interview for jobs in the right project management market space that best fits you!

Many external resources, models, examples and anecdotes are provided for your consideration throughout this book. It is up to you to select and use the tools that best fit your situation. Transitioning from the military is never easy, but if you can find some nuggets within this book that help, then the book will have fulfilled its purpose. Finally, just know you are not alone. Many have come before you and have made the transition. Draw upon others to assist you with their transitional stories through GR8Transitions4U.com. Just like the case study below, you can and will be successful in the next exciting phase of your life – plan on it!

CPT Gaetano (Guy) Simeti
Realizing the Roadmap

CPT Gaetano (Guy) Simeti, enlisted in the Illinois National guard out of high school based on advice of his father, a former army officer, believing that the service would provide good life experience and college tuition. Guy wisely used the National Guard college money and the G.I. Bill to attend a local university. During his junior year of college, Guy made the decision to join the Reserves Officers' Training Corps (ROTC) and subsequently obtained a commission, as an active duty engineer Lieutenant in 2006. He liked the idea of being an Army engineer because he was told "Engineers learn to build stuff and you get to blow stuff up."

After going to his first duty assignment, Guy quickly realized as a Lieutenant it was more about planning, managing, tracking and updating stakeholders (more senior officers) on the status of your personnel who "build and blow stuff up." During his first command experience, Guy became aware of the need to manage his career when his boss stated that the way to get ahead was through seeking personal development opportunities. Subsequently, Guy became aware of a recommendation for engineers to pursue the Project Management Professional (PMP®) credential, as discussed in an Army publication (DA Pam 600-3).

After serving as the operations officer for the Directorate of Public Works in Kuwait for a year, Guy realized the magnitude and challenge of managing projects in an overseas environment. This was also his first experience gaining the satisfaction of seeing projects completed. After returning to MacDill Air Force Base in Tampa, his new boss provided Guy some mentorship and recommended he seek out opportunities to make himself marketable, not just in the military, but also in the civilian world. After going to the education center on base, Guy was told about freely available Project Management Institute (PMI) PMP®

learning modules on the Army e-Learning program. He quickly began the modules with the intent of enhancing his personal competencies.

Unfortunately, in 2014, Guy was facing a reduction in force. He realized that a 20 year military career may not be available to him, and immediately began to prepare himself for the best career transition possible. He became a PMI member, joined the local chapter, and began attending PMI Tampa Bay chapter meetings. Through this first external military networking experience, he received encouragement and support from fellow chapter members and PMPs at the meetings. This encouragement kept Guy focused and moving forward during this mentally challenging period. In the interim period, Guy continued studying and preparing for the PMP® exam.

Not long after Guy passed the PMP® exam, Guy was informed that he would have to exit the service. Disappointed, he regretted that he had not started working to prepare earlier on areas such as the graduate record exam, putting money away in the thrift savings plan, and setting up a LinkedIn profile.

Today, Guy is busy turning lemons into lemonade. At the time of this publication, he is diligently working on a personal transition plan. He looks at the nine months to execute this plan before the requirement to depart the service, as a gift. Guy is taking every opportunity to set himself up for success and transition into his next career with the highest probability of success and the least amount of stress. Guy desires to expand his network, polish his resume, take further certifications (Lean Six Sigma), while concurrently looking for a great career, potentially in project management. Two things are for certain, there is life after the military, and Guy is doing the right things to ensure success in his next career.

Appendix

Appendix A – Lexicon

This Lexicon provides a few military terms and definitions with associated commercial project management terminology. The project management definitions are derived from multiple sources, to include the PMBOK®, Project Plus and Wikipedia.

Military/Project Management Lexicon

MILITARY TERM/ REFERENCE	MILITARY DEFINITION	PROJECT MANAGEMENT	PROJECT DEFINITION
Mission or Operation ADP 5-0 (FM 5-0)	Operations generally involve military action or the accomplishment of a strategic, operational, or tactical, service, training, or administrative military mission.	Project	A temporary endeavor undertaken to create a unique product, service, or result.
Mission Statement JP 1-0	A short sentence or paragraph that describes the organization's essential task(s), purpose, and action containing the elements of who, what, when, where, and why.	Project Scope Statement	The description of the project scope, major deliverables, assumptions, and constraints

MILITARY TERM/ REFERENCE	MILITARY DEFINITION	PROJECT MANAGEMENT	PROJECT DEFINITION
Operations Order FM 7-8	An executable plan that directs a unit on how to conduct a military operation	Project Management Plan	The document that describes how the project will be executed, monitored, and controlled.
Commander's intent JP 3.0	A clear and concise expression of the purpose of the operation and the desired military end state that supports mission command, provides focus to the staff, and helps subordinate and supporting commanders act to achieve the commander's desire result without further order, even when the operation does not unfold as planned.	Strategic Plan	Document used to communicate with the organization the organizations goals, the actions needed to achieve those goals and all of the other critical elements developed during the planning exercise.
Mission Command System ADP 6-0 (FM 6-0)	The arrangement of personnel, networks, information systems, processes and procedures, and facilities and equipment that enable commanders to conduct operations.	Enterprise Project Management	Way of thinking, communicating and working, supported by an information system, that organizes enterprise's resources in a direct relationship to the leadership's vision and the mission, strategy, goals and objectives that move the organization forward
Operational environment	A composite of the conditions, circumstances, and influences that affect the employment of capabilities and bear on the decisions of the commander.	Enterprise Environmental Factors	Conditions, not under the immediate control of the team that influence, constrain or direct the project, program or portfolio.

MILITARY TERM/ REFERENCE	MILITARY DEFINITION	PROJECT MANAGEMENT	PROJECT DEFINITION
Prudent Risk **ADP 5-0** **(FM 5-0)**	A deliberate exposure to potential injury or loss when the commander judges the outcome in terms of mission accomplishment as worth the cost.	Risk Acceptance	A risk response strategy whereby the project team decides to acknowledge the risk and not take any action unless the risk occurs.
By-pass criteria **FM 7-20,** **FM 100-15**	A measure during the conduct of an offensive operation established by higher headquarters that specifies the conditions and size under which enemy units and contact may be avoided.	Risk Avoidance	A risk response strategy whereby the project team acts to eliminate the threat or protect the project from its impact.
Troop leading procedures **ADP 5-0** **(FM 5-0)**	A dynamic process used by small-unit leaders to analyze a mission, develop a plan, and prepare for an operation.	Project Management Process	The management process of planning and controlling the performance or execution of a project.
Paragraph 5, **OPORD** **ADP 5-0** **(FM 5-0)**	Command and Signal (formerly Command and Control)	Communications Management Plan	A component of the project management plan that describes how, when and by whom information about the project will be administered and disseminated.
Mission Orders **ADP 6-0** **(FM 6-0)**	Directives that emphasize to subordinates the results to be attained, not how they are to achieve them.	Charter	Mission and Goals for a Program or Project
Science of Control **ADP 6-0** **(FM 6-0)**	Systems and procedures used to improve the commander's understanding and support accomplishing missions.	Monitoring and Controlling	The process of tracking, reviewing and reporting the progress to meet the performance objectives defined in the project management plan

MILITARY TERM/ REFERENCE	MILITARY DEFINITION	PROJECT MANAGEMENT	PROJECT DEFINITION
Joint Doctrine **JP 1-02**	Fundamental principles that guide the employment of forces of two or more services in coordinated action toward a common objective. It will be promulgated by the Chairman of the Joint Chiefs of Staff, in co-ordination with the combatant commands, services, and joint staff.	PMBOK ®- Project Management Body of Knowledge	A set of standard terminology and guidelines for project management.
Joint Operation Planning and Execution System. **JP 1-02**	An Adaptive Planning and Execution system technology. Also called JOPES	PMBOK - Planning Process Group	Those processes required to establish the scope of the project, refine the objectives and define the course of action required to attain the objectives that the project was undertaken to achieve.
Unity of Command **JP 3-0**	The operation of all forces under a single responsible commander who has the requisite authority to direct and employ those forces in pursuit of a common purpose.	Organizational C-Level	Organization Chief Executive Officer (CEO), Chief Financial Officer (CFO), Chief Information Officer (CIO) and Chief Technology Officer (CTO)
Unity of Effort **JP 1-0**	Coordination and cooperation toward common objectives, even if the participants are not necessarily part of the same command or organization—the product of successful unified action.	Program and Portfolio Standard Body of Knowledge®	Strategic Alignment of goals at either the Program, Portfolio or Organizational levels

MILITARY TERM/ REFERENCE	MILITARY DEFINITION	PROJECT MANAGEMENT	PROJECT DEFINITION
Control **ADP 6-0 (FM 6-0)**	The regulation of forces and warfighting functions to accomplish the mission in accordance with the commander's intent.	Earned Value Management and formulas for Schedule and Cost variances and indexes	Comparing actual performance with planned performance, analyzing variances, and assessing trends to effect process improvements, evaluating possible alternatives and recommending appropriate corrective action as needed.
Authority **ADP 6-0** **(FM 6-0)**	The delegated power to judge, act, or command.	Project Charter	A document issued by the project initiator or sponsor that formally authorizes the existence of a project and provides the project manager with the authority to apply organizational resources to project activities.
Execution **ADP 5-0** **(FM 5-0)**	Putting a plan into action by applying combat power to accomplish the mission.	Project Phase: Monitoring and Controlling	Overseeing all the tasks and metrics necessary to ensure that the approved and authorized project is within scope, on time, and on budget so that the project proceeds with minimal risk.
DP or Decision Point **ADP 5-0** **(FM 5-0)**	A point in space or time the commander or staff anticipates making a key decision concerning a specific course of action.	Milestone or Gate	A significant point or event in a project, program, or portfolio.
Horse Blanket	Lay down on paper a course of action.	Project Schedule	An output of a schedule model that presents linked activities with planned dates, durations, milestones and resources.

MILITARY TERM/ REFERENCE	MILITARY DEFINITION	PROJECT MANAGEMENT	PROJECT DEFINITION
Back Brief **FM 6-0**	Briefing by subordinates to the commander to review how subordinates intend to accomplish their mission	scope definition process	Ensuring that all stakeholders understand the scope through a collaborative approach in an effort to minimize scope creep during project execution
AAR - After Action Review **FM 6-0**	Guided analysis of an organization's performance, conducted at appropriate times during and at the conclusion of a training event or operation with the objective of improving future performance.	Close Procedures - Lessons Learned	The knowledge gained during a project, which shows how project events were addressed or should be addressed in the future with the purpose of improving future performance.
Task Organization	It is the process of temporarily allocating your forces (and determining the command and support relationships) in order to set the conditions for achieving a particular mission.	Project Team	Team level that received value by virtue of delivering a project to its completion.

Appendix B – Rosetta Stone

The Rosetta Stone
(Translating Your Military Experience to the PMI Certification Application Process)

	Phases of Military Planning (Service Specific)								
INITIATE	X								
PLAN		X	X	X	X	X			
EXECUTE				X			X	X	
MONITOR & CONTROL	X	X	X	X	X	X	X	X	X
CLOSE									X
Navy Planning (NWP 5-01)	Commander's Estimate		Planning	Directives			Orders	Supervison of Planned Action	Hot Wash/AAR
Army Troop Leading Procedures (ATP 3-21.8)	Receive Estimate	Issue Warning Order	Make Tentative Plan	Initiate Movement	Reconnoiter	Complete the Plan	Issues OPORD	Supervise	Hot Wash/AAR
Military Decision Making Process	Receive Estimate	Mission Analysis	COA Development	COA Analysis	COA Comparison	COA Approval	Orders Production		Hot Wash/AAR
Marine Corps Troop Leading Steps (CPL 0301)			Begin Planning	Arrange for Reconnaissance	Make Reconnaissance	Complete the Plan	Issue the Order	Supervise Activities	Hot Wash/AAR
Joint Operational Planning and Execution System [Deliberate Planning] (Users Guide for JOPES)	Initiation	Concept Development	Plan Development	Plan Review	Supporting Plans Development				Hot Wash/AAR
Joint Operational Planning and Execution System [Crisis Action Planning] (Users Guide for JOPES)		Crisis Assessment	COA Development	COA Selection	Execution Planning		Execution		Hot Wash/AAR

*Air Force Planning is deliberately integrated with JOPES.
Augmented JOPES instruction with Detailed Air Force guidance is provided in AFI 10-401.*

Appendix C – Certifications by Certifying Organization

CERTIFICATION
Categories: **A** = Agile **P** = Project **G** = Government **S** = Specialty; can be any specialized or enhanced certification

CATEGORIES	
	**AACE	International**
	web.aacei.org/certification/certifications-offered/professional-certifications
S	Certified Cost Professional (CCP)
S	Certified Estimating Professional (CEP)
S	Earned Value Professional (EVP)
S	Planning & Scheduling Professional (PSP)
	**AAPM	American Academy of Certified Project Managers**
	certifiedprojectmanager.org/certification.html
P	MPM Master Project Manager™
P	CIPM Certified International Project Manager™
S	PME Project Manager E-Business™
S	CEPM Certified Executive in Project Management
A	AAPM Accredited Agile Project Manager
S	CPRM Certified Project Risk Manager or Certified Risk Analyst®
S	CPP ™ Certified Product Planner™
S	COG-PM - Certified Oil and Gas Project Manager™
P	CPC Certified Project Consultant©
S	CCPC Certified Construction Project Consultant™
S	CIPPM Certified International Project Portfolio Manager™
S	CPPM Certified Project Portfolio Manager™
S	DBA Designated Business Analyst
S	CEVMA ™ Certified Earned Value Management Analyst™
A	ChPM Chartered Agile Project Manager™
S	CRMO Certified Risk Management Officer™
	**AIPMM	Association of International Product Marketing and Management**
	aipmm.com/
S	Certified Product Manager
S	Certified Product Marketing Manager
S	Agile Certified Product Manager and Product Owner
	CompTIA
	certification.comptia.org/home
P	CompTIA Project+
	**DAWIA	Defense Acquisition Workforce Improvement Act**
	icatalog.dau.edu/onlinecatalog/CareerLvl.aspx?lvl=1&cfld=9
G	Program Management level I
G	Program Management level II
G	Program Management level III
G	Information Technology I
G	Information Technology II
G	Information Technology III
	**FAI	Federal Acquisition Institute**
	www.fai.gov/certification/program-and-project-managers-fac-ppm
G	- Level I
G	- Level II
G	- Level III
	**GAQM	Global Association for Quality Management**
	gaqm.org/certification/project_management
P	Associate in Project Management (APM)™
P	Professional in Project Management (PPM)™
S	Certified Project Director (CPD)™

io4pm
www.io4pm.org

P	Project Manager Accredited CertificationTM
S	Program Manager Accredited CertificationTM
S	Project Quality Manager Accredited CertificationTM
S	Product Manager Accredited Certification™
S	Service Manager Accredited Certification™
S	Business Analysis Accredited Certification™
S	Project Manager TrainerAccredited Certification™
S	Project Manager Coach Accredited Certification™

International Association of Project Managers
www.iapm.net/en/certification/levels-of-certification/overview/

P	Certified Junior Project Manager
P	Certified Project Manager
A	Certified Junior Agile Project Manager
A	Certified Agile Project Manager
S	Certified Senior Project Manager
A	Certified Senior Agile Project Manager
P	Certified International Project Manager

IPMA I International Project Management Association
www.ipma.world/individuals/certification/

S	Certified Projects Director (Level A)
S	Certified Senior Project Manager (Level B)
P	Certified Project Manager (Level C)
P	Certified Project Management Associate (Level D)

PMI I Project Management Institute I
www.pmi.org/certifications

P	Certified Associate in Project Management (CAPM)®
P	Project Management Professional (PMP)®
S	Program Management Professional (PgMP)®
S	Portfolio Management Professional (PfMP)
S	PMI Professional in Business Analysis (PMI-PBA)®
A	PMI Agile Certified Practitioner (PMI-ACP)®
S	PMI Risk Management Professional (PMI-RMP)®
S	PMI Scheduling Professional (PMI-SP)®

Prince 2
www.axelos.com/best-practice-solutions/prince2

P	Prince2 Foundation
P	Prince2 Practitioner
P	Prince2
D	Prince2 Agile

Scrum Alliance
www.scrumalliance.org/

A	Certified Scrum Master (CSM)
A	Advanced Certified ScrumMaster (A-CSM)
A	Certified Scrum Product Owner (CSPO)
A	Advanced Certified Scrum Product Owner (A-CSPO)
A	Certified Scrum Developer (CSD)
A	Advanced Certified Scrum Developer (A-CSD)
A	Certified Scrum Professional (CSP) for ScrumMasters (CSP-SM)
A	Certified Scrum Professional (CSP) for Developers (CSP-D)
A	Certified Scrum Professional (CSP) for Product Owners (CSP-PO)
S	Certified Team Coach (CTC)
S	Certified Enterprise Coach (CEC)
S	Certified Agile Leadership (CAL)
S	Certified Scrum Trainer (CST)

Appendix D – Salary Considerations

Congratulations! You've just received the job offer! Now it's time to consider the salary and benefits being offered. Salary negotiations are tricky and can be a sensitive subject for both you and the employer. Therefore, you need to be prepared.

Let's say the salary sounds low. What do you do? Sixty percent of American workers take the salary and accept the job. You can do the same. However, you may desire to think it over. If they desire to hire you, thoroughly understand the total offer as it relates to your personal circumstances. Ask your future employer lots of questions. If they get irritated or illusive and the salary is low, maybe the job is not the right fit.

The best offense is the superb defense. Be prepared with the knowledge to know what the fair and equitable salary would be for you. Remember you will not have the opportunity to renegotiate for at least a year. Here are some considerations on salary research you should perform to be best prepared for salary negotiations.

1. Research a fair salary and thoroughly understand the benchmarks for your position. You should find all the salary information available for the position you are applying and arm yourself. You will need to spend adequate time conducting research on average salary ranges for similar jobs in the industry and your local area. Check out websites like Payscale.com, Salary.com or Glassdoor.com.

2. Decide on an appropriate salary range for yourself. To determine a realistic salary range, forego any thoughts about how many kids you have in college, your boat payment, or your upcoming European vacation. Instead, research and calculate your appropriate salary based on the research that you have conducted and then your personal situation. It is also good practice to identify your "can't live with" point. Think about the reasons why you would not be willing to accept a lower amount.

3. Understand the total compensation package. This means to look at benefits such as: bonuses, medical, dental, education, and 401K match. With regard to benefits, some companies offer great benefits and others do not! Talk to anyone that has been in the job market for a while and they will tell you there are significant differences in companies and their benefits such as PTO (Paid Time Off - or the equivalent of military leave).

   If a bonus is part of the package, make sure you have the program in writing and understand exactly how the bonus program works. Further, if PTO is important to you and the company is rigid about the number of days or hours off, ask if you can buy more. Look at the total cost of your medical, dental, short-term and long-term disability insurance. How much life insurance will you need? Can you buy more? Is the insurance a good value compared to your other life insurance policy?

   All these total compensation elements are essential to review. Consider the benefits package, but don't forget to study the location for tax, commuting, parking, housing, crime and schools. Remember, you are in control and only you will accept the offer. There are areas of the offer you can negotiate and other areas you cannot.

You must study the benefits and consider how to negotiate. When it comes to understanding total compensation, most look at three components: direct financial compensation, indirect financial compensation, and non-financial compensation. Also, there are personal quality of life issues to consider. Here are a couple of real-world examples.

SCENARIO 1: After leaving active duty and joining the reserves, John took a huge cut in pay and went to work for another company. People thought he was crazy. Turns out he was crazy like a fox. The new job was close to home. He saved 50 miles a day on his vehicle, reducing tolls, fuel, maintenance cost, while recovering 75 minutes a day from his commute. His dental coverage for his son's braces was running out just before his job transition. With the new job, he received a new dental plan, which paid the remaining 2-year orthodontic bill. His educational benefits and 401k were both better. Finally, within two years he was making the same salary as before and his total compensation was much higher.

SCENARIO 2: Mike took a well-paying defense contractor position in nearby state. He received a $42K uplift in wages over his military pay and $5k sign on bonus which he used toward the move. But his new company's medical insurance was very expensive, and the deductibles were high. Accustomed to paying neither city nor state tax; Mike was simultaneously being forced into a higher federal tax bracket. Housing was more expensive; his commute was 50 minutes longer each day and he had to pay to park. Bottom line, with the very nice salary bump, he thought he was making a lucrative financial move for his family. He was wrong!

These two accounts are based on real events. As you look at your job offer, closely review the total compensation. If you are being given an excellent offer for your personal situation, then skip the negotiation and take the offer. However, if you want the job and the offer seems a little off based on your research, don't be intimidated. Remember, salary and benefits can be negotiated with a little personal finesse.

Be assured, you are highly desirable. Employers want you! Take some time for research and you will make a great choice for your family as you transition from the military.

Appendix E – Personal Strategic Road Map

Personal Strategic Road Map v1.6

Vision: Obtain A Project Management career that meets or exceeds my expectations

Mission: Develop a course of action to create a satisfying and financially lucrative transitional outcome.

Transition Date:
RoadMap Initiation Date:

IMPROVEMENTS

ASSESSMENT RESULTS ➤ Areas for Change/Improvement from Star Chart results outside the pentagon

	Change / Improvement # 1	Change / Improvement #2	Change / Improvement #3	Change / Improvement #4
1. Environmental/Spousal				
2. Characteristics				
3. Timing				
4. Skills				
5. Market Place	☐ Commercial ☐ Contract ☐ Civil Service			

VISION

VISION: Based upon your reading and the five assessment areas above, restate your job objectives to include some or all of the following: Job place/location (CONUS/OCONUS, state/city, timeframe, marketplace focus, salary range, possible positions, risk level you are willing to take, Industries, and any other considerations

YOUR VISION:

GOALS & ACHIEVEMENT

GOALS: Pick most important improvement areas from above you want to focus on, depending on level of complexity, learning, or duration (i.e., school).

* List: goals, align which Assessment area it ties, year/quarter/month expected to achieve, and present your achievement path (how you will get to your goal and possible steps if necessary

PRIORITY	GOAL STATEMENT	ASSESSMENT TIE	PATH TO ACHIEVING GOAL	YEAR/QTR/MO TO ACHIEVE (personality set)	ACHIEVED ?
GOAL # 1	enter goal here	Environment — Characteristics — Timing — Skills — Market Place	enter steps.....		YES / NO Reschedule or no longer need? Date
GOAL # 2		Environment — Characteristics — Timing — Skills — Market Place			YES / NO Reschedule or no longer need? Date
GOAL # 3		Environment — Characteristics — Timing — Skills — Market Place			YES / NO Reschedule or no longer need? Date
GOAL # 4		Environment — Characteristics — Timing — Skills — Market Place			YES / NO Reschedule or no longer need? Date

ATTEST

Date of Next Review:

Signature: _____ Date: _____

Spouse Signature: _____ Date: _____

GrMilitaryPM.com
©Copyright 2014

Acknowledgments

This book would have been impossible without the tremendous collaborative effort. They say that it is good to have differing viewpoints, although this book could have been finished in half the time if one of us would have taken a back seat every now and then.

On a serious note, our diversity drove innovation. Constantly knocking ideas together and honing the product gave us a tremendous feeling of satisfaction, knowing that through this book we will increase the success of our transitioning servicemen and women. We are thankful for this inspiration.

It is always difficult to narrow a list of acknowledgments, let alone for two coauthors. A tremendous number of people have affected our learning and writing process. Great thanks are due to these friends and colleagues for their encouragement and desire to see this work completed so that it can fulfill its original intent, providing guidance to those in transition. While we want to thank everyone, it is always a possibility that someone is missed. But, you know who you are, and we are forever humbled for the friendship and grateful for your support.

Throughout this journey, we became aware of the tremendous power of friendship and comradery. Many military and corporate friends were extremely excited to assist in developing this work. Our brothers in arms felt compelled due to their kinship and understanding of the challenges associated with the military transition. Their common belief in the sacrifices made by the military, while in service to the country provided daily inspiration for this effort.

This first book was a journey to mix what we both know, project management and the military. On the project management and business side, this book would not have gotten very far if not for the enthusiasm and networking by John Watson and John Stenbeck. Getting to know John Stenbeck was nothing short of phenomenal, as he offered guidance and insight not normally given to authors so green. His desire and ability to share knowledge and lessons were a gift that continues to give today. Through John and others, we are compelled to 'pay it forward', both through the completion of this book, and those looking to make the world a better place through the sharing of knowledge.

Writing and editing assistance proved invaluable. Keith Jones and Dennis Barletta marched every step of the way. Cam Miles, AKA 'the nitpicker', provided support nothing less than stupendous.

Hal and Pat Hicks believed in this work from day one. YC and Rachel Parris' significant professional connections and assistance proved invaluable throughout the effort. Thank all of you for your review and encouragement.

It is through many volunteer positions with PMI, particularly through Sandy's bond with Peggy Stepanick, and others in the PMI Leadership Master Class that provided continual support and innovation. Wanda Curlee and Brian Grafsgaard provided enduring encouragement and are unbelievable friends and colleagues, carrying the water during times of overload. Also, thanks to Darcy Hotchkiss, providing her 'just do it' personality tied to both business and military acumen.

We extend a very humble thank you to the folks that have given us their project management stories. We are grateful for their desire to assist us, as this book would not be the same without the incorporation of their personal accounts.

Finally, to Kellie, Darien and Logan, Jayson and Bob – a very special thank you for your support, talent and understanding during the challenging times associated with the development of this work.

May God continue to bless our Service-members!!

Jay and Sandy

End Notes

Chapter 1

1. "ARCHIVES: Hurricane Katrina 2005 News Media Coverage,"
   YouTube, January 11, 2013, www.youtube.com/watch?v=eHcyC5sc_so
   (accessed July 25, 2019).

2. Dr. Woody Woodward, "Why Veterans Make Good Project Managers,"
   Fox Business News, January 30, 2012, www.foxbusiness.com/features/
   why-veterans-make-good-project-managers (accessed July 25, 2019).

3. "Talent Gap: Project Management through 2020," Project Management
   Institute, March 2013, www.pmi.org/learning/thought-leadership/
   pulse/talent-gap-2020 (accessed July 25, 2019).

Chapter 2

1. Shane Christopher, "Why Are Employers Seeking Military Experience,"
   G.I. Jobs, April 28, 2014, www.gijobs.com/why-are-employers-seeking-
   military-experience/ (accessed July 25, 2019).

2. "Veteran Jobs with Military Friendly Employers 2019," Military
   Benefits, 2019, militarybenefits.info/veteran-jobs-with-military-
   friendly-employers/ (accessed July 25, 2019).

3. Society of Human Resource Managers, "Employing Military
   Personnel and Recruiting Veterans, What HR can do," SHRM, June
   23, 2010, www.shrm.org/ResourcesAndTools/hr-topics/benefits/
   Documents/10-0531%20Military%20Program%20Report_FNL.pdf
   (accessed July 25, 2019).

4. Moira Alexander, "6 Traits of Highly effective Project Managers," CIO, August 4, 2017, cio.com/article/2433916/project-management-six-attributes-of-successful-project-managers.html (accessed July 25, 2019).

5. Ryan Guina, "How Big Should Your Emergency Fund Be?", The Military Wallet.com, April 10, 2019, themilitarywallet.com/how-big-should-your-emergency-fund-be/, (accessed July 25, 2019).

Chapter 3

1. Woodward, "Why Veterans Make Good Project Managers."

2. Project Management Institute, *A guide to the Project Management Body of Knowledge (PMBOK Guide) Sixth Edition,* (Project Management Institute, 2017), 23.

3. Project Management Institute, *A guide to the Project Management Body of Knowledge (PMBOK Guide) Sixth Edition*, (Project Management Institute, 2017), 4.

4. Project Management Institute, *A guide to the Project Management Body of Knowledge (PMBOK Guide) Sixth Edition,* (Project Management Institute, 2017), 11.

5. Wikipedia, "Project Portfolio Management," en.wikipedia.org/wiki/Project_portfolio_ management (accessed July 25, 2019).

6. Project Management Institute, *A guide to the Project Management Body of Knowledge (PMBOK Guide) Sixth Edition*, (Project Management Institute, 2017), 11.

7. "The State of the Project Management Office (PMO), pmsolutions, 2014, pmsolutions.com/reports/State_of_the_PMO_2014_Research_Report_FINAL.pdf (accessed July 25, 2019).

8. "PMI's Pulse of the Profession In-Depth Report: The Impact of PMOs on Strategy Implementation," *Project Management Institute,* November 2013, pmi.org/learning/thought-leadership/pulse/impact-pmo-strategy-in-depth (accessed July 25, 2019).

9. Ronda Bowen, "Top 11 Benefits of Becoming PMP Certified," *Bright Hub Project Management*, July 31, 2013, brighthubpm.com/

certification/57121-benefits-of-the-pmp-credential/ (accessed July 25, 2019).

10. CompTIA, certification.comptia.org/certifications/project (accessed July 25, 2019).

11. "Program Management Professional (PgMP) Examination Content Outline," *Project Management Institute*, April 2011, pmi.org/-/media/pmi/documents/public/pdf/certifications/program-management-professional-examination-content-outline.pdf (accessed July 25, 2019).

12. "PMI Code of Ethics and Professional Conduct", *Project Management Institute*, December, 1997, pmi.org/about/ethics/code (accessed July 25, 2019).

13. "Defense Acquisition Workforce Improvement Act (DAWIA)," *Defense Acquisition University*, dau.mil/faq/Pages/Certifications-Programs.aspx (accessed July 25, 2019).

14. "DAWIA Certification & Core Plus Development Guides," Defense Acquisition University, http://icatalog.dau.mil/onlinecatalog/CareerLvl.aspx (accessed July 25, 2019).

Chapter 4

1. Tranette Ledford, "The Best Jobs: Government Employee or Government Contractor?," *ClearanceJobs,* July 25, 2010, news.clearancejobs.com/2010/07/25/the-best-jobs-government-employee-or-government-contractor/ (accessed July 25, 2019).

2. Tranette Ledford, "The Best Jobs: Government Employee or Government Contractor?"

3. Tranette Ledford, "The Best Jobs: Government Employee or Government Contractor?"

4. "Best Places to Work Agency Rankings - large," *Partnership for Public Service*, 2017, bestplacestowork.org/rankings/overall/large (accessed July 25, 2019).

5. "Special Hiring Authorities for Veterans ", Federal *Special Hiring Authorities*, fedshirevets.gov/job-seekers/special-hiring-authorities/#content (accessed July 25, 2019).

6. "Pay & Leave: Salaries & Wages," *Office of Personnel Management,* opm.gov/policy-data-oversight/pay-leave/salaries-wages/salary-tables/19Tables/html/DCB.aspx (accessed July 25, 2019).

7. "Benefits and Pay for Federal Employees," USA.Gov, February 02, 2015, usa.gov/benefits-for-federal-employees (accessed July 25, 2019).

8. Beyond My Ken, "The Pros and Cons of Working in the Public Sector," Living Rich Cheaply, 2013, livingrichcheaply.com/2013/08/22/the-pros-and-cons-of-working-in-the-public-sector/ (accessed July 25, 2019).

9. JJohn Cibinic, Jr. and Ralph C. Nash, Jr., *Administration of Government Contracts, Third Edition,* (The George Washington University, Government Contracts Program, National Law Center, Washington D.C., 1995), 3.

10. Tranette Ledford, "The Best Jobs: Government Employee or Government Contractor?"

11. Beyond My Ken, "The Pros and Cons of Working in the Public Sector."

12. "401(k) Plans," *Internal Revenue Service,* October 14, 2014, irs.gov/retirement-plans/401k-plans (accessed July 25, 2019).

13. The Consultants' Corner, "The Stark difference between private and public sector ERP implementations, *Panorama Consulting Solutions,* September 13, 2013, panorama-consulting. com /?s=The+ Stark +difference+between+ private+and+public+sector+ERP+ implementations (accessed July 25, 2019).

14. "Report of the Federal Salary Council Working Group," *GovernmentExecutive.com*, September, 2014, https://www.govexec. com/media/gbc/docs/pdfs_edit/101714kl2.pdf (accessed March 19, 2020).

15. Ronda Bowen, "Top 11 Benefits of Becoming PMP Certified."

16. Particia Lotich, "5 Employee Benefits Required by Law," Thriving Small Business, thethrivingsmallbusiness.com/employee-benefits/ (accessed July 25, 2019).

17. "PricewaterhouseCoopers, LLP why work here," *Vault,* vault.com/company-profiles/accounting/pricewaterhousecoopers-llp/why-work-here-benefits/diversity-and-inclusion (accessed July 25, 2019).

18. Best Places to Work Agency Rankings - large," *Partnership for Public Service.*

Index

The Military Transitioning Series

The Transitioning Military Series helps service members evaluate and understand their potential to transform themselves into a marketable commodity within both public and private sectors. Each career-based book enables the translation of military experience to the commercial world. Read and use each of these books as a reference to guide during your transition. Insight is provided for those seeking the most satisfying job beyond their military career, with real-world success stories. Companion Guides for each book are now also available through GR8Transitions4U.

A unique combination of features offered through this book series include:

- Career Mapping and Translation
- Commercial Market Exploration
- Transitional Preparedness
- Individual Assessments
- Personal Strategic Roadmap

Interested in another career field? Check out our other books on career field transition for the military:

| **Logistician** | **Information Technology** | **Cybersecurity** Professional | **Combat Arms** Professional |

Jay Hicks and Sandy Lawrence are dedicated to providing insight and guidance for those looking to transition successfully from the Military with the least amount of stress. Both Jay and Sandy speak around the U.S. in support of transition as well as career field insight, and are available for conferences, podcasts, webinars, and training. For more information on upcoming events and new releases, visit: GR8Transitions4U.com.

Made in the USA
Las Vegas, NV
01 August 2021